STUDIES IN ORIENTAL RELIGIONS

Edited by Walther Heissig
and Hans-Joachim Klimkeit

Volume 42

1998

Harrassowitz Verlag · Wiesbaden

Women and Religion in Japan

Edited by
Akiko Okuda and Haruko Okano

Translated by Alison Watts

1998
Harrassowitz Verlag · Wiesbaden

Publication of this book was supported by a grant of Förderverein japanisch-deutscher Kulturbeziehungen e.V., Köln.

The series STUDIES IN ORIENTAL RELIGIONS is supported by

Institute for Comparative Religion, Bonn University
Institute for Central Asian Studies, Bonn University

in collaboration with

Institute for Advances Studies of World Religions, Carmel, New York
Institute of History of Religion, Uppsala University
Donner Institute, Foundation of Åbo Akademi University, Åbo, Finland
Institute of Oriental Religions, Sophia University, Tokyo
Departement of Religion, University of Hawaii
Instituto Italiano per il Medio ed Estremo Oriente, Roma

Die Deutsche Bibliothek – CIP-Einheitsaufnahme

Women and religion in Japan /ed. by Akiko Okuda and Haruko Okano.
Transl. by Alison Watts. – Wiesbaden : Harrassowitz, 1998
    (Studies in oriental religions ; Vol. 42)
    Einheitssacht.: Shūkyō-no-naka-no-joseishi <engl.>
    ISBN 978-3-447-04014-9

© First edition: Synukyou no nakano joseisi.
Edited by Akiko Okuda and Haruko Okano. Seikyusha Co. Ltd., Tokyo 1993

© English Edition: Otto Harrassowitz, Wiesbaden 1998
Otto Harrassowitz GmbH & Co. KG Kreuzberger Ring 7c-d, D-65205 Wiesbaden,
produktsicherheit.verlag@harrassowitz.de

ISSN 0340-6702
ISBN 978-3-447-04014-9

Contents

Translator's Note

Alison Watts

What is feminism? The word itself and as an ideology, it can mean many things to many different people, with class, race, age, education, religion and culture all being influential factors. The breadth of intellectual inquiry and experiences of the Japanese women authors in this volume show that there is no single template which can be used to identify the roots of women's subjugation, rather that the causes are as diverse as the religions and cultures that have shaped the often so-called homogeneous society of Japan.

In translating this volume I have had to call upon the resources of many people to answer my questions about the various religions represented in Japan. Thank you to all of them and also particular thanks to Leanne Eames for translating the chapter on Soka Gakkai.

Please note that all Japanese names confirm to the conventional order in Japanese of family name first.

Introduction

Okuda Akiko

Feminism is not a monolithic system of views. Whilst in the process of becoming absorped into society it has come to incorporate many different opinions, although despite this diversity there is one aim on which feminists are in accord, and that is the need for the elimination of patriarchy. Patriarchy is a keyword of feminism used both in the West, the Third World and Japan, but the word itself has various interpretations and without the existence of a common understanding, eliminating it is something easily talked about but not so readily achieved.

The meaning of patriarchy in the west was derived in the context of societies based on ancient Hebrew and Roman models, but in Japan "there has never existed an actuality which conforms to the western concept of patriarchy,"[1] and it was the *ie*, or household system of samurai society, which shaped the meaning. It is therefore impossible for Japanese feminists to unquestioningly accept a Western feminist critique of patriarchy in the Japanese context, but in order to develop a proper critique for themselves, it is first necessary to explicate the nature of patriarchy in Japan.

There have been other investigations of the subject, but they have been weighted to an economic perspective, examining the role of women labourers and women's status under a capitalist economy, and ignoring almost all other political, ideological and social factors. De Beauvoir, Kate Millet and other western feminists have attached great importance to Christianity as being chiefly instrumental in the oppression of and discrimination against women, but for Japanese feminists there is something lacking in this point of view. The concept

---

[1] Seki Hirono, Yaban toshite no Ie Shakai, Ochanomizu Shobo, Tokyo, 1987.

that "God the Father is useful for legalising a patriarchal society"[2] is a common perception amongst western feminists, which does not necessarily apply to the Japanese situation.

In Islamic society too, believer in social democracy and Egyptian feminist writer Nawal El Saadawi, while taking the position that economic factors and not religion are the fundamental cause of womens oppression, and even while recognising in her explication of patriarchy that religion cannot be separated from the political system and is used to perpetuate patriarchy,[3] still holds in common with western feminists the view that religion is a large factor in this.

In Japan however, it was the patriarchal community structure of samurai society and the concomitant *ie*[4] system of the military community with its resultant ideology, which played a main part in the perpetuation of patriarchy. The argument that religion had therefore almost no power to influence patriarchy in Japan is very powerful. Certainly there were no circumstances which could have permitted opposition to a 'God the Father', but nor could it be said that either Buddhism or Confucianism performed the same role historically and socially as Christianity or Islam. In place of a monotheistic God, Japanese society has a tradition of eight million deities. The concept of gods living in mountains, rivers, grasses or trees, and the idea that anyone - the Emperor, his subjects or even war criminals - can easily become a god, is a religious conception of a wholly different nature to the notion that 'there can be no other God but I' of Christianity or Judaism.

That being the case, the question then arises as to whether or not there is absolutely no connection between religion and patriarchy in Japan. Research into women's history has shown that at least up until

---

[2] Mary Daly, Womanspirit Rising, Harper and Row, New York, 1979. Japanese translation by Okuda Akiko and Iwata Sumie.

[3] Nawal El Saadawi, Eve no Kakureta Kao (The Hidden Face of Eve, Zed Press, London, 1980), Miraisha, Tokyo, 1988.

[4] The *ie* is a concept and unit of Japanese society that denotes a household group based on family connections and is almost always headed by a male. Translator's note.

the Kamakura period (1185-1333) the status of women was not so low. If this is so, why is it then that within the culture of the *ie*, women suddenly became generally subordinated in position and in character. And, moreover, why was *ie* culture, originally a part of samurai ideology, not confined only to samurai families: how did it come to affect women of all classes and why were there unprecedented cases throughout Asia of the status of women dropping dramatically? When the original *ie* system crumbled, why did the ideology continue to live on in peoples consciousnesses? The answers to these questions cannot be found solely in economics. Body and spirit are joined and inseparable, it is impossible to abstract either one. We should therefore direct our attention to the spiritual climate of Japan which gave rise to such circumstances.

The intrinsic irresponsibility and group collectivism of the 'Emperor religion' is a distinct characteristic of Japan's spiritual climate. There is an endless series of bribery and corruption scandals involving politicians; the Sagawa Kyubin scandal[5] and the way in which it was handled by politicians is a typical example of this. Politicians seem not only to have no sense that violating the law is a crime, but also no consciousness of the people as sovereign. Intent on increasing their personal wealth they forget that they are supposed to be spokesmen for the people, and when there is a storm of criticism, they simply pull in their necks and wait for it to blow over, affecting an attitude that is the very antithesis of democracy. The people, however, while saying on the one hand that not much can be expected of politicians, also do not follow through with their anger by expressing it at the ballot boxes. Hence similar types of scandals occur over and over again.

Chun Kwangne points out in her chapter that the shameless attitude to the comfort women issue and war responsibility stems from the same roots. What is the reason for the great contrast in attitudes of Germany's reflection and soul-searching on the criminal behaviour of

---

[5] In 1992 the manager of the delivery service Tokyo Sagawa Kyubin was found to have bribed politicians in exchange for favours. Translator's note.

Nazis during the war, compared to Japan's evasion of the forced labor and comfort women issues as if they had never existed?

Takeuchi Yoshiro maintains that the reason for the ambiguity and lack of responsibility pervasive in the Japanese spiritual climate, is the lack of a transcendent principle.[6] A transcendent principle relativises all power and authority of the present world and is the conceptual framework which provides tools for criticism. With an integral awareness of a transcendent principle, people have the ability to relativise themselves, thus enabling self-criticism and self-reflection. The leaders of Japan exhibit no self-criticism or self-accusation over crimes they have committed, and the anger of the people eventually tapers away because there is no established transcendent principle which functions as a standard for the taking of responsibility. Ambiguous and indifferent attitudes toward war responsibility, and politicians' methods of taking responsibility for bribes amongst other things, lie in the lack of such a transcendent principle within Japanese society.

Religion in Japan has been greatly affected by such a spiritual climate; if religion is mentioned then people think of sects like the United Church or The Science of Happiness, or if not then they say that Japan is a non-religious society. Whichever the case, there is a general perception that religion has no personal relevance. In spite of this, however, the 'Emperor religion' mentioned previously has permeated society; 55% of the population actually believe in God or Buddha, according to an NHK public opinion poll.[7] Faiths which promise benefits in this life such as divination, fortune-telling, charms and protections, are predominant amongst young people. This phenomenon would seem at first glance to be unrelated to religion, but bearing in mind that the number of believers in Shinto and Buddhist faiths rise as age increases, it is possible that believers of 'benefits-in this-world' faiths will convert to Shinto and Buddhist beliefs as they grow older. Customs such as visiting graves, observing anniversaries

---

6   Takeuchi Yoshiro, Imi e no Kawaki, Chikuma Shobo, Tokyo, 1988.
7   Gendai Nihonjin no Ishikozo, Nihon Hoso Shuppan Kyokai, Tokyo, 1991.

of deaths, prayer meetings and visiting shrines at New Year have deeply penetrated people's everyday lives, with even people who do not ordinarily worship Shinto or Buddhism having religious funerals. In view of this, the word 'non-religious' would not appear to express the real situation. As Clifford Geertz writes, "religious symbols and ceremonies form one part of the cultural ethos, and prescibe the deepest values held by society and the people in that society,"[8] and so even unconsciously, religious characteristics have a deep influence on people's spirits and values.

Despite the definite existence of religion, there is no perception as such because in the past and in the present, religion has not always functioned in the role of religion. That is to say, there was no original universal religion with a transcendent principle established in Japanese society, not to mention the fact that all faiths have been confused by the 'Emperor religion'.

This lack of a transcendent principle also affects the structure of Japanese patriarchy. Its reality is ambiguous and therefore identifying sexual discrimination is difficult. Unlike the male power centered structures of western patriarchy symbolised by 'God the Father', the nature of Japanese patriarchy might be called 'maternal' because of the obscurating, all-embracing imperial system with which it is imbued. Elucidation of the nature of this 'maternal patriarchal' system is therefore necessary.

It is well known that women are not regarded equally within religions, and from a feminist point of view, the perspective is surprisingly similar for all religions. Christianity, for example, apportions the blame for man's fall into sin, onto Eve. Buddhism teaches that women with sins must first become 'metamorphosed men' in order to attain Buddhahood. Discriminatory language towards women is plentiful in St. Pauls Epistles, a driving force in the formation of the Christian Churches (although recent research suggests that the author of the epistles was not necessarily only Paul).

---

[8] Clifford Geertz, Religion as a Cultural System in Reader in: Comparative Religions, ed. William Lessa and Evan Vogt, Harper and Row, New York, 1972.

For feminists in western societies where Christianity constitutes the cultural backbone, patriarchy is synonymous with the Christian Church. In response they have developed an equally strong and radical critique of the Christian Church, stressing the return to a female God and the feminine aspects of Jesus' image, because they see men as oppressors and rulers of a system which forces women into submission to a sole transcendent 'God the Father'.

But religion is a pledge of fidelity to an abstract God rather than the powers of this world, and as such its existence can constitute a threat from the state's point of view. Therefore state authorities have used and involved themselves in religions as a means of maintaining order in society. Hence from very early on religions with the power of anarchy were institutionalised so as to maintain control and order, thus linking them to the affirmation of the status quo. If there is no reform in the status quo, then the only way in which people can be given a sense of liberation is to have their attention focused on a world other than the present one, which is why in all religions so much importance is attached to 'salvation in heaven'. Then a pattern is created in which the worse the discrimination and oppression of this world becomes, the more that despairing people look to be saved by religion. In this way religion has conspired in the oppression and discrimination of women, a situation which still continues today.

Looking at the long history of women's oppression by religion like this, it may seem rather strange then to attempt to combine religious values with feminism. Many people think that religion is only an impediment to feminism and could not possibly be of any advantage in the liberation of women. Former ardent Catholic Mary Daly reached the point of asserting a post-Christian Church because she believes the Christian Church is anti-feminine beyond saving. Should religion be disavowed entirely however, and are the large number of women fascinated by religion nothing more than simply gullible fools?

It is paradoxical that when oppressed and discriminated people become conscious of a transcendent existence, they find courage to dauntlessly resist the irrational. The women close to Jesus described in the New Testament were like this, and there are many examples of people who however low and without hope, find the verve and drive to live life positively through their belief in God. In various countries of Central and South America where injustice is rampant and conditions of the poor intolerable, liberation theology spread by Catholic priests gives people hope for the same reason. The spread of Buddhism during the Kamakura period also had a similar immeasurable effect on the populace in Japan.

It is therefore necessary to be cautious about this duality in religion, the twin aspects of oppression and liberation which it contains, and a simple outright rejection would be to overlook its great strengths. The concepts of human rights, freedom, equality and humanist philosophy considered to be born of modern western thinking, have their roots in a universal religion. If anything, it is through a universal religion with a transcendent principle that strength will be drawn to overcome the patriarchism which has become a feature of the Japanese spiritual climate.

For this purpose it is necessary to examine and establish a critque of the way in which existing religions have oppressed women and the effect this has had on the formation of the Japanese spiritual climate. Furthermore, if it is that male centered religions emerged at the same time as patriarchy came into being, then an elucidation of feminine spirituality before such religions, is important, and by so doing it will be possible to clarify the distinctive features of Japanese patriarchy.

With this in mind the "Feminism, Religion and Peace Group" was inaugurated in 1986 to examine and form a critique of religion from a feminist perspective, and all contributors to this book have some connection to this group. We were encouraged by the examples of feminist theologies put into practice by women in Christian countries and coloured Christian women's creation of a womanist theology, and so started this group with the hope of planting a feminist religion in the Japanese soil. It takes courage to criticise one's own religion while still maintaining a committment to it, and we could draw strength from the example of western feminist theologians and from other group members with the same concerns. The feminist slogan "sisterhood is powerful" became a reality for us.

In the same way that there has long been religious conflict between Christianity and Judaism, Catholics and Protestants, in Japan too there has been conflict between the Buddhist Nichiren Sect and Soka Gakkai. The dispute between orthodoxy and heteredoxy is endless and it is easy to become conservative and dogmatic. As a result, dialogue which rises above religions and sects is rare. Several years ago in England, when John Hick broke from Christian Church centred doctrine to propose a religion of pluralist principles that preaches the way of a variety of Gods, there were many people who reacted with shock and could not accept it at the time. However, women who have been excluded from the power structure and status system within religions have the potential to be much freer from the conservative and sectarian mentality which reacted against such a proposal. Our group members come from various backgrounds such as the Christian Church, Buddhist, new religions, post-religion and atheist, so in a sense this could be called the first step towards realisation of a pluralistic religion, although we try to replace the word 'religion' as much as possible because it is contaminated for most of us.

In this book it was possible to examine only a small part of the various religions in Japan, and so it could not be said that this is still not a sufficient elucidation of Japanese patriarchy. In some chapters the criticism of religion is very strong, others investigate 'femininity' before religion and test the regeneration of women's religion which has been struck from male history; therefore the positions on religion are varied. However, these are only differences in focus of interest and as such are illustrative of the diversity of feminism, not essential differences.

Through a thorough scrutiny of the seemingly incongruous themes of feminism and religion, we hope to clarify a little more the relationship between women and the Japanese spiritual climate, and bring to Japanese feminism something of a spiritual viewpoint which has been lacking up to now. There is a long way to go to reach our goal but this book is one small step towards it.

A Feminist Critique of Japanese Religions

Okano Haruko

1. Introduction

The twentieth century has been an epoch-making period in women's history because of the growth in solidarity which has developed into a global movement. There have also been momentous developments in the field of religious history, as charges by Christian liberation and feminist theologians that religion was a means for the acceptance and legitimisation of sexual, class and minority discrimination, prompted a radical reexamination of the meaning and role of religions to begin simultaneously in many cultural disciplines. In this sense then, the twentieth century can be labelled an era of 'renewed modernisation', analogous to the series of religious reforms in the Reformation. It is through such critique and re-examination of the existing value system that potential for change opens up, and if feminists, theologians, ecologists, intellectuals and other anti-discrimination activists can achieve this without being forced to compromise, then the re-empowerment of women becomes possible.

If religion is complicit in the discrimination that occurs in the various realms of human activitiy, then it is not just sexual discrimination, but other types such as class and race, which are also affected. Thus achieving the conditions for women to realise their potential is linked to solving problems of class, minority and various other discriminations. In this sense then, I believe that women can demonstrate genuine strength and significance by joining in movements of resistance against the powers and authorities who discriminate against the weak.

Amongst feminists themselves there are diverse interpretations of religion, and numerous debates on topics such as the necessity of religion, religious cultural devices, and metaphysical systems indispensable to human existence. In the afterword (The Future of

Feminism and Religion), I will discuss my own opinion on the meaning of religion for Japanese society. Whatever their position on religion, however, there are probably no feminists who would deny the fact that within the patriarchal framework of Japanese society, the values of Shinto, Buddhism and Confucianism cast deep shadows.

The question arises at this point as to whether sexual discrimination is a strategy or structural necessity of religion in the first place. Is there a different underlying cause for discrimination in each separate religion, or is there some hidden broad-based cause of a completely different nature. Throughout Japanese history there have been women who have boldly fought against the injustices and contradictions of women's lives, yet at the same time still managing to maintain strong religious affiliations (see chapters by Iwata Sumie, Okuda Akiko and Haga Akira). Many of them, however, were swallowed up in the wave of androcentric society. What is it that they sought, and who or what was the opponent they fought against.

Western feminist theologists have as a common starting point the Bible, edited to focus on men, and a Church formed by the patriarchal dynamics which justified and entrenched women's subordination. Japanese feminism has to contend with basically the same problems of sexual discrimination, but the phenomena of women's subordination is of a completely different nature to its western counterpart. The real means of subordinating Japanese woman is not necessarily the individual male who represents her as head of the *ie* (household), but lies somewhere between the *ie* and the state structure - which are of course presided over by men. And because individual men are also subordinate to the system, the problem of sexual discrimination in Japan becomes multi-layered and thus opaque. The phenomenon known as *Nihonteki* (Japaneseness), further clouds the issue because of the indivisibility of the state structure itself and religion.

In the following sections I will examine and comment on Shinto, which has been employed as a religion for preserving the status quo of the system, as well as Buddhism, Confucianism and new religions, which have all been integrated into society in a typically Japanese style and made to function for the preservation of the status quo.

2. Shinto

Somewhat surprisingly, the simple folk religion of Shinto, which is basically a combination of primitive spiritual beliefs and ancestor worship, has from the beginning of Japanese history consistently helped to sustain the charisma of a pure Imperial line, in tandem with a nationalistic view of the world. Even in the high-technology society of modern Japan, Shinto has sustained the original natural communal life that developed naturally and forms the mothering framework in which Japanese locate themselves. Individuals believe optimistically that within the bounds of this folk religious natural community, they are guaranteed happiness and peace, and are living in an homogeneous society where there is no differentiation between the world and self, others and self. During the process of civilising Latin and Germanic societies of ancient Europe, the Christian Church dismantled tribal communities based on blood ties, and the accompanying group mentality which did not differentiate the self from the world. Similarly in Arabia, various original folk religions were replaced by Islam, and in India too there was a period, albeit short, during which Buddhism flourished to answer the spiritual needs of a societal structure which had become conscious of individuality.

In Japan, on the other hand, the imported religions of Buddhism, Confucianism, Taoism and Christianity did not have the force necessary to dismantle the Shintoistic communal spirit. On the contrary, through the medium of ancestor worship so essentially familiar to Japanese peoples spirituality, the Shinto communal structure strengthened the sense of family community and facilitated the promotion of an ideology of the state as an expanded form of the *ie*, the basic household unit around which communities were formed. The absolute and sacred nature of the Japanese nation was moreover affirmed through the placing of an Emperor, descended from the gods, at the peak of the social structure, although Buddhism and Confucianism also played a part in legitimising and strengthening the formation of this ideology. The distinguishing feature of Japanese society as a pseudo-national community according to Kawai Hayao,[1] can be understood as an all-embracing maternal principle. In contrast to the holy/profane, good/evil, above/below dichotomies of the west, in which weaker or negative elements are suppressed, Japanese society is based on a family principle which tends to harmonise by embracing everyone indiscriminately and extolling the absolute equality of all members of this family. In this sense, modern Japanese capitalism is an offshoot of Japanese Shinto state ideology. As long as one stays within the bounds of this mothering social order, peace and happiness are guaranteed, just as children are embraced equally at the bosom of their mother. Thus Japan has developed into a civilised nation where, as Isaiah Benderson has marvelled, 'water and safety are free' and there is universal education extending to even the most remote areas.

Throughout history there have been a number of people who tried to cut such maternal ties and forge an autonomous path for themselves. On the whole, however, the issues of individual ability and individuality are problematic in Japanese society, where not being too different is in fact a condition of survival. Men who have the urge to strongly express their individuality face the same degree of social resistance as women trying to overcome sexist role stereotypes. The social fabric is also tightly bound because everything in Japanese society is understood in terms of relationships and connections, an outlook underlined by the five human relationships and five cardinal virtues of Confucian thought. Consequently everyone, both men and women, is expected to devote themselves to the nation or some kind of organisation; be it man or woman, superior or inferior, everyone is compelled to sacrifice themselves, resulting in a general feeling of victimisation. This psychic structure, in which everyone is a victim and robbed of their autonomy, is one reason why it is difficult to objectify sexism. Over 120,000,000 Japanese cannot all continue as infants at the mothering breast of the state or company, and some must emerge to take responsibility. The ultimate problem for Japanese feminism is how to develop the individual identity and will to exercise

---

[1] Kawai Hayao, Bosei Shakai Nihon no Byori, Chuokoronsha, Tokyo, 1976.

independence in a people who have always entrusted everything to organisational structures.

Despite the influence of this maternalistic principle, the hierarchy and structure of institutions in the national community were undisputedly developed by men in an androcentric society. It is my opinion that the driving force for such patriarchal development in Japanese society originates from the promotion of centralisation by an imperial family conscious of political power. As the *Kojiki*[2] and *Nihon Shoki*[3] testify, the source of the imperial family's power is derived from the divine authority of the ancestral deity, Amaterasu (see chapter by Kono Nobuko). Because Amaterasu is the ancestral goddess of the imperial family and the Sun Goddess who governs the universe, it is commonly believed that she is the highest god in the pantheon. As told in the *Kojiki* and *Nihon Shoki*, however, Amaterasu was not the topmost god nor even a supreme god. In the *Nihon Shoki*, the supreme god who commands the others is not Amaterasu but a male god called Takamimusubi, a fact which reflects the values and particularly strong political consciousness of the compilers of the *Nihon Shoki*. According to the legends described in both books, however, in contrast to Takamimusubi whose divine nature is ambiguous, it is Amaterasu who is most vividly portrayed as the actual leader of the pantheon of gods in *Takamagahara*, the High Celestial Plain where the deities reside. There is also the example of Himiko, the ancient female ruler of Japan described in the *Gishiwajinden*.[4] Himiko was adept at a form of shamanism and enjoyed a great following, but it was her brother who actually administered politics,

---

2 The Kojiki (Record of Ancient Matters) is Japan's oldest extant chronicles, recording events from the mythical ages of the gods up to the early 7th century. Translator's note.

3 Nihon Shoki (Chronicle of Japan) is the oldest official history of Japan covering events from the mythical ages of the gods up to late 7th century. Beginning in the Kamakura period (1185-1333), it also came to be viewed as a sacred Shinto text. Translator's note.

4 The section of the history of the Chinese Wei Dynasty (220-265) which describes the countries of Wa (Japan) and tells of the female ruler Himiko to whom almost all Wa countries are said to have given allegiance. Translator's note.

although he is barely mentioned in the *Gishiwajinden*. This fact taken together with the portrayal of Amaterasu, would seem to suggest the form of government in ancient Japan. Even when Susanoo, younger brother of Amaterasu, commits numerous reckless acts, Amaterasu does not rebuke him in the slightest or even punish him, she instead shows tolerance and permits everything. Religious psychologist Matsumoto Shigeru has pointed out that the all-forgiving and tolerant Amaterasu, and by extension the community of *Takamagahara*, are an embodiment of the Jungian maternal principle.[5] It is worth noting that the deity revered as the ancestor of the imperial family is not the mother god Izanami, who gave birth to the islands of Japan and exalts in both the power of life and destruction, but Amaterasu, the pure-hearted virginal god with a fund of unlimited forgiveness and the psychological symbol of an all-embracing mother. In a patriarchal society striving for discipline, it is the noble Amaterasu who is chosen to attest to the sacredness of the imperial family and becomes the universally desired ideal of woman. These are the same kind of patriarchal values which have elevated the simple Mary from the status of eternal virgin and mother, to that of a Holy Mother raised up to heaven by God. And in the same way that the cult of the Virgin Mary has deep connections with the issue of sexism, so too does the role of Amaterasu function as a blind to cover sexism in Japanese society. It has been conjectured that, as with goddesses revered in other religions, Amaterasu also originally fulfilled a simple double role; mother of the god of rice plants and priestess.

From the time of recorded history onwards there has been a centralised state with the Emperor at its pinnacle; but with Shinto as the foundation of the system's authority, it became structured around patriarchal dynamics and was transformed in the process. Despite Amaterasu being the Emperor's ancestral goddess, it was the god Takamimusubi who was revered at the centre of the *Ritsuryo* state, a system of centralised autocracy based on comprehensive legal codes

---

5   Matsumoto Shigeru, Fuseiteki Shukyo Boseiteki Shukyo, Tokyo Daigaku Shuppan Kai, Tokyo 1987.

that came into being in the late 7th century. *Ritsuryo* law itself is based on the premise that all rightful authority is derived from a sovereign who is above the law.

Amaraterasu's symbol, the mirror, was originally enshrined in the sleeping quarters of the Emperor, but in the course of unification by the imperial family during the reign of Emperor Sujin, it was removed to Ise in what is now Mie Prefecture, and worshipped by the Emperor's daughter. What is the significance of this transfer to Ise of Amaterasu, who had up to then shared the same roof as the Emperor? To borrow the words of Jungian psychology again, this deeply mythically-tinged incident becomes in effect matricide by the Emperor - the rejection of the archetype mother within who has given birth and nurtured while also at the same time engulfing - and is nothing other than the securing of ego and the first step towards autonomy. From a historical and religious point of view, this was the point at which the delineation between politics and religious ceremony in the imperial family became established. From a feminist standpoint it was the first step taken by the patriarchal state to exclude female power from the centre. Thus, in an act symbolic of the patriarchal disposition of the imperial family, Takamimusubi was enshrined, and replicas of the sacred objects of Amaterasu were worshipped by the Empress and princesses at the Imperial court. The ceremonies for Amaterasu were transferred to Ise, where she became a daughter to the successive Emperors instead of a sister as before, and from then onwards patriarchy was established in the imperial family.[6]

In this way the Emperor's rule split into the two realms of 'ceremonial' and 'political' along gender lines, a split which signifies the transition through patriarchal dynamics of the parallel rule of Hime and Hiko in ancient Japanese tradition, to the schema of Hiko = master = politician, and Hime = assistant = priest.[7] From descriptions of Himiko in the *Gishiwajinden*, and tales of female leaders mentioned in

---

[6] See Kuratsuka Akiko, Fujo no Bunka, Heibonsha, Tokyo 1979 and Okano Haruko, Die Stellung der Frau im Shinto, Harrassowitz, Wiesbaden, 1976.

[7] Hime is a term of address for a female god and Hiko for a male god. Translator's note.

the *Kojiki, Nihon Shoki* and local histories, it can be inferred that at this stage the parallel rule of Hime and Hiko had not yet been segregrated into ceremony and politics. The establishment of Ise Shrine, the origin of the Hime and Hiko political/ceremonial split, was a major turning point in the history of Japanese women. Hime was prised away from the ancient parallel ruling structure to become the shrine maiden who acted as the Emperors representative serving the ancestral gods in rural Ise, and this patriarchal state structure survived until the 14th century.

The transformation in power relationships between Hime (Amaterasu) and Hiko (Takamimusubi) in the community on *Takamagahara*, and the Emperor's Hime (princess who served at Ise Shrine) and Hiko (Emperor), is reflected in the organisation of Shinto ceremonies central to the *Ritsuryo* system of government under a national system of administration. During the Taika Reforms of the second half of the 7th century, Shinto shrines throughout the country came under the administration of the *Jingikan* (Department of Shinto Affairs). In the course of such bureaucratisation, Shinto priests also became government employees. These public servant priests carried out their duties by performing prescribed ceremonies and calling down the gods at will, making redundant the uncertain possessions and revelations of the *miko* (female shamans) who had up to then carried out this task. This was the first step in the process of modernising Shinto and the Japanese state, and gradually through rationalisation and regulation of the various forms of human activity, irrational and weaker elements were eliminated and suppressed. Although women priestesses made a comeback after World War II because of the shortage of men, it has nevertheless been men who have been the major players in the history of Shinto since the Middle Ages. Women's activities were restricted to the world of folk religion, on the outskirts of society where the scalpel of modernisation could not reach. The reason why the archaic folk religion of Shinto can continue to sustain meaning in modern Japan, is found in the coexistence of androcentric state ceremony with the folk religions represented by women. Shinto was also not threatened by the introduction of Buddhism because it was internalised separately, both for the community's spiritual peace, and as a means of strengthening the authority of Shinto. Thus it was adopted and adapted in a peculiarly Japanese style which upheld the existing status quo.

3. Buddhism

Buddhism, which is supposed to dismantle the group consciousness into individual consciousness in the context of Japan, came to incorporate secular values and became a defender of the system, thus depriving itself of the opportunity for the self-denial and self-relativisation essential for genuine modernisation and maturity.

The question of sexual discrimination inherent in the ideas of Gautama Buddha, is an issue that should be examined in conjunction with developments in philological research, however it can be said that the teachings of Buddha were plainly edited, with discriminatory ideas becoming accepted in the process of evolving and establishing doctrine. In regard to this I would like to refer to Okoshi Aiko's lucid critique *Sabetsu Suru Bukkyo*,[8] which focuses on how defense of the ruling system came to bureaucratise Japanese Buddhism, the consequent influence on women's history, and the anomaly of how monks who have supposedly renounced the world can have their own *ie*.

In the mid 6th century, ascetic clerical Buddhism was brought to an ancient Japan where shamans prayed for fertility and regeneration. Pro-Buddhist policies were vigorously opposed by the powerful Mononobe and Nakatomi families of the Yamato Court. Reading the *Nihon Shoki*, it seems that the reason given for their rejection of Buddhism was the fear of provoking the anger of the native gods. Soon after a second burning of Buddhist temples and images, there was a plague in which the Emperor and one of the Mononobes suffered from smallpox and many people died. In the *Nihon Shoki* the

---

[8] Okoshi Aiko, Sabetsu Suru Bukkyo, Hozokan, Kyoto, 1990.

cause of this misfortune is attributed to the act of burning Buddhist temples and images, an understanding based on the animist characteristic of Shinto faith.

Three women, reminiscent of Himiko and the *miko* of ancient times, were the first to serve at the Buddhist temples of Soga no Umako (?-672, the powerful court patron of Buddhism) as a means of coping with the social anomaly of a new religion. Buddhism was accepted not on account of its superior doctrine, but because of the expectation of benefits to be reaped from miracles occurring in the present world, expectations which pivoted on the concept of *tenbyoenju* (get well and live long). It was, however, transformed into a new ideology for strengthening the community by incorporating Buddhist doctrine into the Seventeen Article Constitution promulgated by Prince Shotoku in 604, which exhorted the importance of *Wa* (harmony). The ancient Japanese, whilst accepting a world-renouncing Buddhism which fundamentally rejected all existing points of view of the times, modified Buddhism's essential nature, and thus further consolidated the natural maternalistic community which fulfilled the conditions of *Wa*.

During the short seventy years after Buddhism was introduced to Japan from the Korean kingdom of Paekche, it came to be regarded as equally effective as native gods for invoking miracles, and was integrated into the *Ritsuryo* state as a new type of religion by which peace of the nation could be sustained through *Wa*. Thus from the beginning, Buddhism's evolution in Japan was slanted toward preserving the status quo and for the benefits it could give in this world, subjugating the issue of individual religious desires. Japanese style transformations of Buddhism are clearly evident in the authorising system of the central administrative bureau that prohibited monks and nuns from proselytising, and even controlled their original mendicant lifestyle.[9]

---

[9] According to the fifth article of the Yoro Code drafted in 718, a legal code of ancient Japan which served as the basis of Japanese government until the early 10th century.

As Buddhism became increasingly bureaucratised from the latter half of the 10th century to the end of the 11th century, the practice of barring women began at conservative mountain temples such as Hieizan and Koyasan, and administrative temples such as Todaiji. The background to this practice, the acme of sexual discrimination, was the negative perception of women as a sinful sex, undoubtedly fostered by the notion of 'five hindrances' and 'three obediences' repeatedly mentioned in the Mahayana Sutras (see chapter by Nakano Yuko). This was not the only factor, however, and there is evidence that the idea of excluding women was mooted in at least one other place. Sometime around the 10th century, Kukai, founder of the Shingon sect, pleaded in a work called *Goigo* that the exclusion of women was an opportunity to preserve the precepts of the clergy.[10] The tradition of excluding women, begun as a means of maintaining discipline amongst the monks, became a complete expulsion of women through the paradoxical rationale that 'it reveals the holiness of the mountain.' Furthermore, because the powerful temples charged with upholding the political system were also closely connected to Shinto and consequently the Shinto concept of blood impurity, their shunning of blood impurity gave further impetus to the tradition of excluding women. Buddhist ascetics and the desire to preserve national peace through religion bear a great part of the blame for the frequent appearance of negative images of women in literary and religious writing, and the various restrictions on women in religious life from the middle ages onwards.

Why is it then that despite these anomalies the exclusion of women has continued to recent times? The reason can be found in the existence of *satobo*, another factor obfuscating sexual discrimination.

Special villages, known as *satobo*, were constructed for the mothers and sisters of monks at the base of holy mountains where it was taboo for women to go. These *satobo* functioned as both a hometown where the parents resided and as *ie*, a household of which monks were the

---

[10] See Okano Haruko, Bukkyo no Joseikan (II) - Nihonteki Tenkai, in Jissen Joshi Daigaku Bungakubu Kiyo, vol. 33, Tokyo, 1991.

head. So in effect, while the monks lived atop the mountain, where holiness was preserved through the exclusion of women, devoting themselves to prayers and training and carrying out various religious affairs in service of the state, the women were down below in the *satobo* doing menial tasks like sewing clerical robes and washing to support the monk's religious life.[11] The *satobo* also served as a refuge for women in need of help and a home to those who had renounced worldly life. In entering the *satobo* the lives of women under the protection of a monk were at least guaranteed secure. Their idea of ultimate salvation was to be nursed in their dying hour by a monk, perhaps their relative, be cremated and succeed at last in reaching the holy peak by having their ashes laid to rest in its precincts, regarded as being akin to entering Paradise. In short the religious sanctuary area taboo to women was recognised as fulfilling an important social function in being the means by which women, the socially weak, might find salvation in the *satobo* on its outskirts, an intersection of contact between the holy and the lay. There were also religious and political imperatives for these taboo areas, namely the preservation of Buddhist precepts, acceptance of Shinto taboos and avoidance of impurities for the sake of preserving the peace of the nation.

Thus the *satobo* served as the world of a Buddhist style saint. It is notable that they also came to develop characteristics of a folk religious sacred area, with many originating from the tradition and mystique surrounding mothers of famous monks. When a mother who had lived a religious life at the base of the mountain under the protection of her son was nursed to a peaceful death by him, she came to be worshipped as a patron saint of safe birth and nursing. Some well-known examples are the mothers of Saicho (767-822, founder of the Tendai sect) and Kukai (774-835, founder of the Shingon sect).[12] This tradition of achieving salvation as a woman through becoming the mother of a virtuous monk, is the same as much of the folklore on

---

[11] Nishiguchi Junko, Onna no Chikara - Kodai no Josei to Bukkyo, Heibonsha, Tokyo, 1987
[12] Nishiguchi Junko, ibid.

dying, which maintained that women could be saved even in a female form, through becoming a mother. In a similar vein, the traditions of Japanese Buddhism teach that gender and sexuality can be overcome, thus enabling the salvation of women, by either renouncing worldly life or becoming a man through metamorphosis. The further women were away from the formal religion of Japanese Buddhism concerned with upholding the status quo and preserving peace, the more that they were supported on the margins of society by faith in an ancient folk mother god and were at the very least able to lead a liberated existence as mothers.

Thus salvation and discrimination are intertwined, making it difficult to perceive the phenomenon of female taboo as sexual discrimination.

In addition to the 'pure' priests on the mountaintop, leading ascetic lives while possessing a *satobo* at the base, there were also other monks who married, established their own *ie* and led otherwise ordinary lives in society while keeping up an appearance of renouncing the world. The marriage of monks became officially recognised during the Meiji period (1868-1912), however it is possible to trace the existence of married monks from the regulations regarding monks and nuns in the Yoro Code of 718.

There is an underlying maternal principle in Japanese Buddhism which appeases and is accepting of everything, so that apart from the clergy who were directly charged with defending the state and preserving peace through Buddhist law, there was no development of a morality which values judging actions strictly according to religious precepts. Hence it was possible for many priests who were serving in a temple to establish their own *ie*, a practice which also led to the establishment of the custom of passing custodianship from father to son in hereditary succession, instead of from teacher to disciple as it is supposed to be.

Ie have always existed in the Jodo Shin sect (True Pure Land sect) because of a revelation received by the founder, Shinran (1173-1263), while in the Rokkakudo temple in Kyoto, that the sect should be structured around husbands and wives. Shinran and other Jodo Shin priests, Zonkaku and Rennyo, accepted the intermingling with women, but in spite of the existence of *ie* in the sect they continued as always to preach to wives of monks and female followers the concept of metamorphosis for women; inconsistencies which justified traditional sex roles and are now coming under indictment by feminists. From the 12th century onwards the number of monks increased, but after the Meiji Restoration they were deprived of their public standing as the clergy increasingly came to be regarded as a profession rather than a way of living. Until then, however, the wives of monks were acknowledged only on a de facto basis and lived in the shadow of their husbands, who were supposedly renouncing the world.

Based on Shinran's perception of himself as neither monk nor layman, the *ie* of the monks, although illegal, was tacitly recognised and came to be an important aspect of religious life in the Jodo Shin sect. In pre-Kamakura period (1192-1333) Buddhism the masculine principle can be epitomised as: mountain top = male (monk) = defense of country = holy; while the corresponding feminine principle would be: village = female = secular. The *ie* of the Jodo Shin sect gained a new religious meaning through pursuing the sublation of this holy/wordly dualism. Shinran used a self-deprecating word for the word 'I' as an indication of the deep sense of wrongdoing with which he had established an *ie*, but in the Japanese context it was nevertheless a cocoon of gender-based role divisions.

4. Confucianism

By the mid-fifteenth century temple ordinances regulated the different sects and lives of Buddhist monks down to the smallest detail, so much so that priests became in effect like public servants. At about this time too the *danka* system, requiring everyone to register as parishioners at Buddhist temples, was implemented by the shogunate as a means of exposing Christians and other underground believers labelled dangerous, and generally keeping the entire populace under surveillance. Funeral and memorial services had to be conducted by temples, thus transforming Buddhism into the ceremonialised form known as 'funeral Buddhism.' Buddha himself would not know how it is that monks who were supposed to be striving for deliverance from worldly attachments through training, came to be professional conductors of memorial services for ancestors! Gautama Siddhartha did not venture any comment about the world after death because he basically denied it existed. Whatever the case, the sweeping adoption of ancestor memorial services was a religious policy welcomed by the establishment as a means of reinforcing the *ie* system.

In addition to assimilating Buddhism, the shogunate regime was also interested in Confucianism as an ideology for bolstering the feudal system. More an academic discipline than a religion, Confucian studies were considered to be a study of ethics. The core of these ethics are the five cardinal virtues and five cardinal principles, moral rules that govern the five human relationships (ie. king and subject, father and child, husband and wife, older brother and younger brother, friend and friend). It has often been pointed out that the Chinese understanding of the hierarchy of relationships, ie. filial piety of a child towards parent and loyalty of a subject to the king, functioned from the beginning in Japan as establishment ideology in which loyalty to the nation was given priority.[13] Loyalty to the state was regarded as of paramount importance, therefore attention was focused on the *ie* as a pillar of the state structure. Originally three of the five human relationships were virtues related to familial connections, a fact which the state used to its advantage in strengthening the *ie* system by ethical means, and employing the logic of ancient regimes in strengthening the ties of the *ie* to the state.

With the exception of the virtue of friendship, which comes last in the five human relationships, all relations were understood to be a hierarchy conforming to the natural order. *Jokunsho*, the books of teachings compiled for women by Confucianists in the Edo era,

---

[13] See Fujiwara Seika, Chiyomoto Gusa, for example.

maintained women's complete subordination as a matter of course.[14] The book *Onna Jitsugokyo* published at the end of the 17th century, demanded the complete subordination of women to men and the *ie*, in language devoid of logic and obsessed with the sinfulness and impurity of women, which added to the stigma already created by Buddhism.[15]

Through the melding of Buddhism and Confucianism, women's status was becoming increasingly lower, and about the time that circulation of the *Ketsubon* Sutra gave further impetus to perceptions of womens inferiority and impurity (see chapter by Nakano Yuko), a book criticising patriarchal society was already being written in Italy. The author was a woman called Lucrezia Marinella (1571-1653). In her book she criticised the concept of court rank, one which dates back to Aristotle and greatly resembles the five human relationships; namely the concept that between king and vassal, father and child, and man and woman there exists a hierarchy in the guise of natural law.[16] The final stage of the Renaissance in Italy, from the 16th century to the first half of the 17th century, was an era in which mankind discovered self -identity and the concept of relativising the world was maturing. This comparatively long history of conceptual development was surely a vital period of preparation for western feminism, for which there is no equivalent in Japan.

Reforms were carried out at the end of the 18th century to mend cracks which had begun to appear in the shogunate system. Although promotion of agricultural policies was the main objective, public morals and discipline were also enforced, and paternal rights in the *ie* system promoted as a means of strengthening the political regime. From this period onwards the contents of *Jokunsho* also became reactionary, and since education was deemed as undermining the

---

[14] These books originated in China where they were mainly written by women, but in Japan they were, with few exceptions, written by men. Translator's note.

[15] Kakei Kumiko, Edoki Sanjusha no Jokunshiso ni Miru Haha to Onna, in Bosei wo Tou ed. Wakita Haruko, Jinbunshoin, Kyoto, 1988.

[16] Elisabeth Gössmann (Hg.): Archiv für philosophie-und theologiegeschichtliche Frauenforschung, Bd.2, iudicium Verlag, München, 1985.

virtue of women's obedience, it was concluded that 'no talent is woman's virtue,' thus absolute obedience to husband, father-in-law and mother-in-law were strongly emphasised.

Following the publication of the Japanese translation of Lucrezia Marinera's book in this period, there began to gradually emerge women who levelled criticism against the feudal system that legitimised the injustices of women's lives. The life of Tadano Makuzu (1763-1825) is a vivid example of the conditions and limitations necessary for women to be recognised in men's society at this time.[17] The daughter of Kudo Heisuke,[18] she grew up in an environment surrounded by scholars of Dutch, Chinese and Japanese classics. She displayed a gift for Japanese from an early age and while a young girl expressed the wish to study Chinese classics, a request that was refused by her father. As a member of the Kudo *ie* she married into the house of a powerful samurai family in Sendai, but tragically her younger brother who became head of the Kudo house, died young and the *ie* died with him. Thus did the efforts of half her life come to nothing; namely, to forge connections with a powerful house by marriage and to cultivate womanly virtues for the sake of the *ie*. Once again she felt acutely the insignificance and powerlessness of woman's existence. In despair she wrote a commentary entitled *Dokko* (Solitary Thoughts), in which she cites Dutch and Japanese classics to comment on Confucian ethics that oppress female sexuality, a commentary which opened up a new platform for politics and economics. She sent this to popular Edo writer, Takizawa Bakin, with a request for comments and help with publishing. Although an adherent of Confucianism and known as difficult to please, Takizawa was moved by the diligence of the author who, despite being a woman, he saw as being motivated from the filial duty of ensuring the perpetuation of her father and ancestors' name. *Dokko* was not a

---

[17] See Seki Tamiko, Edokoki no Joseitachi, Aki Shobo, Tokyo, 1980 which touches on Makuzu's ideas from a feminist perspective.

[18] Physician and author of Akaezo Fusetsu Ko, a report which stressed the need for the colonization of Ezo (Hokkaido) to defend it from Russian encroachment. Translator's note.

storybook or fiction, and because it unfolded a theory of social thought that extended to moral training for government and family, Bakin praised her as a woman of talent excelling even that of Murasaki Shikibu and Sei Shonagon, famous Heian authors of The Tale of Genji and the Pillow Book respectively. He applauded her talent as being out of the ordinary, with the words "In body she is a woman but in thought she is a man,"[19] a back-handed form of compliment stemming from a patriarchal tradition that appraises women's intelligence as a masculine attribute - a tradition not unknown in Europe also. There was no intentional spite in Bakin's words, but because such praise is originally used in a favorable sense, it is difficult to recognise the discriminatory mentality behind it, even by the women in question themselves. 'Incisive logic unlike a woman ...' and other such language scornful of women's ability continues to exist even in present society and is tolerated by women.

Makuzu speaks from a Confucian standpoint in the following justification for writing Dokko: "... [I] disregarded the things that a woman ought to think as shameful."[20] This was the topos of humility necessary for a woman to maintain her position in men's society. Even today such humble expressions, whether used in a good or bad sense, continue to oppress women's consciousnesses. The spell of the discriminatory influence of Confucianism in the division of roles in society, must be broken, and it should be affirmed that humility is a mark of maturity, irrespective of gender.

After 10 months or so of corresponding with Bakin, Makuzu inquired about the possibility of her work being published, an inquiry which Bakin thought conceited and took offense. He then promptly wrote two volumes of a refutation of Dokko, called Dokkoron, in the belief that "pride should be broken," and sent it to Makuzu with a letter severing their acquaintance.[21] The content of Dokko was

---

[19] Takizawa Bakin, Dokkoron, in Shin'en sekijusshu 2, published by Hirotani Kokusho Kankokai, Tokyo, 1927.

[20] Takizawa Bakin, ibid.

[21] Takizawa Bakin, Makuzu no Ouna, Toen Shosetsu, in Nihon Zuihitsutaisei 2-1, Yoshikawa Kobunkan, Tokyo, 1973.

certainly incompatible with Bakin's Confucianist values, and the thinking was in some parts prejudiced, dogmatic and immature, but over and above this, it appears that Bakin was impelled into taking such a severe course of action because in pressing for publication of her work, Makuzu deviated from the topos of humility which women are supposed to conform to. Bakin later regretted breaking this friendship, but after receiving the letter and *Dokkoron* from Bakin, Makuzu returned a polite reply and virtually disappeared from the stage of history.

Such a reaction contained elements of Confucian values - to respect one's superiors, and Japanese aesthetics - to break off cleanly. Amongst the known works left by Makuzu, there are a number of collections of essays, travel diary, stories and around 150 poems, but the legacy of her critique of existing religion and conception of the future, which is crystallised in *Dokko*, has not been passed down into the consciousness of women in later generations. When women's individual experiences and statements begin to come alive in other women's consciousnesses, then the continuity of thought that forms a 'women's tradition' can emerge.

As can be seen from the example of Makuzu, existing women's tradition is more of a a dotted line than a continuous one. Makuzu was re-discovered by Ochiai Naobun and Mayama Seika in the Meiji Period, who attempted to place her into a literary category. But due to the consciousness of national polity under direct Imperial rule in the Meiji Period, Makuzu and her life were merely evaluated as the epitome of a woman who had faithfully lived out Confucian ethics. In *Shushin Zukan* (Illustrated Book of Ethics), she is extolled as an exemplary mother who had raised an adopted child.[22]

In the race to modernity it was not understood properly for a long time that Makuzu's defiant assertion of women wanting women's existence as it is to be recognised, would actually strengthen the *ie* system. The reason being that in the totalitarian-orientated state structure, women's independence and autonomy are negative and

---

[22] Nakayama Eiko, Tadano Makuzu, Maruzen, Tokyo, 1936.

threatening factors. As can be seen from the example of Bakin, while the values which evaluate women's superior qualities as being 'masculine' still exist, and while it is only women who are supposed to strive for humility of expression, there can be no possibility of freeing the potential for self-development in women's lives.

5. New Religions

Buddhism attained the status of state religion through the Tokugawa shogunate's policy of temple registration, but in the process the core ceremonies became so formalised as to become mere shells of themselves. In contrast, out of the turbulence that occurred in the the the transition from the Edo to Meiji periods, new religious movements sprang up which could realistically and concretely respond to the religious desires of a populace troubled with poverty, sickness and war. Such popular religious movements formed and developed in protest at established religions, and came to be lumped together under the term 'new religions'. There are many definitions and classifications of new religions, however for the purposes of this paper I will classify them as the comparatively old new religions formed in the last days of the Tokugawa shogunate and Meiji revolution with 2nd and 3rd generation believers, those formed out of the chaos of the second world war, and religious groups formed after the 1970s.

In spite of a diversity of doctrine and activities, the ever-increasing religious groups shared a number of characteristics in common. The first is that the doctrines supporting religious authority, which seem diverse enough at a glance, are in fact derived from existing religions such as Shinto, Buddhism and Christianity. In this sense it could therefore be said that all groups labelled new religions are merely sects of traditional religions.

The second characteristic, is that as existing religious organisations have become too large, new religions have addressed the pressing issues occupying peoples lives to create a pseudo-family community whose structure strongly resembles that of the ie. With the founder as 'parent' and community leaders in the roles of elder siblings, an *ie* is formed as a place of peace for those who have not been helped by traditional religions or social welfare. The values on which perceptions of salvation are based are accordingly realistic, worldly and laicistic.

A third characteristic arising inevitably from the second, is the perception of salvation as being possible in the present life. The image of salvation in new religions is the ultimate liberation and flowering of the whole person, backed by a bodily sense of well-being, to lead a life filled with vitality and joy (known as *yokigurashi* in the Tenri sect).[23] Gratification of human desires and fulfillment of the archaic desire for a blessed and bounteous life are seen as the ideals. Because of these underlying life-affirming values, the core of many new religious groups is magico-religious activities analogous to the shamans of ancient Japanese society who prayed for fertility and regeneration, recovery from illness and a long life.

The fourth characteristic is the active concern with politics in some form or other of many of the groups which have become structured organisations.

Taken altogether it can be deduced from these characteristics that new religions are extremely conservative in nature, are a family for the believers, and are engaged in political and social activities in support of the state society known as Japan.

Followers of all so-called 'new new religions' and 'post-religions' preaching devotion to specific values which emerged or developed since the 1970s, hold values which are undoubtedly different to those of previous religions. The singular focus of their interest is the swift unburdening of poverty, sickness and conflict, and the pursuit of benefits in this world. They search for a purpose to life and desire a mysterious and emotional fulfillment.[24] Yet these sects called 'new

---

[23] Nishiyama Shigeru, Shinshukyo no Genjo, in Rekishi Koron, vol.5, no. 7, Tokyo, 1979.

[24] Ibid.

new religions' also basically have in common the same four characteristics.

New religious sects are based on laicistic and wordly values, and are orientated toward building a family community utopia under the flag of extolling life and fulfillment of desires, within the bounds that it does not disturb the harmony of the hierarchy. They are indifferent to the notion of defiling a sacred world and the spirit of an essentially ascetic quest for truth. Accordingly, there was no foundation for phenomenon such as the barring of women for ascetic purposes and blood impurity, to take root in. According to Inoue Nobutaka, however, comparing new religions to traditional religions in these terms is not necessarily grounds for concluding that new religions do not contain a structure of sexual discrimination.[25] In the tense relationship between the Emperor system and the modern capitalist system, distinctions between men and women based on biological differences can soon be easily transformed into the idea of social gender roles. When separate gender roles are justified by a religious authority, it can be transformed into oppresive sexual discrimination affecting both men and women.

In the oldest of the new religions, women were at the centre of the group and their gender glorified in the form of rejecting existing male centered religions. The first group to be regarded as a new religion was Fujiko, a religious association that reveres Mt. Fuji. At the height of feudalism from the 17th to 18th centuries, it was not only the first religion founded by a woman, but also regarded women's menstruation positively, as an effective social mechanism to ensure progeny. Human equality was amongst the tenets preached by Fujiko, notable because of its orientation towards rectifying the contemptuous notions of women which marked Buddhism and the *Jokunsho*. The succession of women who subsequently founded religions during the last days of the Shogunate were surely pioneers of feminism.

Nakayama Miki, founder of the Tenrikyo sect and known as a god of safe delivery, clearly rejected the notion of women's impurity. Deguchi Nao, the founder of the Omoto sect also interpreted women's

---

[25] Inoue Nobutaka, Shinshukyo to Seisabetsu in Bukkyo 15, Hozokan, Kyoto, 1991.

maternalism positively. They did not, however, evaluate women's worth simply because maternalism is the means of having children, rather they advocated reform of existing society while preaching the sublimation of family love into a brotherly love for humankind throughout the world. Women could also participate in this social reform and so their attention was directed outwards to society. The two founders thought of themselves as having elements of both male and female sexuality, and it appears that this realisation led them to perceive themselves not just as mothers, but as individuals with an identity demanding a full life.

Issonnyorai Kino, the founder of Nyoraikyo, was much more radical. In her original theory entitled *Hemeguri*, she "rejects the hereditary continuation of the *ie*, basis of ties between parent and child, and rejected the status of mother, the means of receiving children."[26] Kino believed that the chief instigator of women's unhappiness was the attachment to children caused by maternalism, and the spell of the *ie* system.

For Miki, Nao and Kino, the desire for salvation as individuals took precedence over making an issue of women's maternalism.[27] They also firmly believed that it is women, at the base of society and thoroughly cognisant of every possible anguish, who will be the saviours of the world. Such a perspective on women is a striking contrast to the enthusiastic praise and admiration of maternalism by Kawate Bunjiro, who founded the Shinto sect Konkokyo also in the period at the end of the shogunate. He was in accord with the women founders on the issue of firmly rejecting the impurity of women, but espoused distinct sex roles of 'men outside, women inside' and stressed the importance of housework and child-rearing for women. Compared to the three female founders who had, based on their experiences as women, overcome gender role stereotyping, and had developed into female

---

[26] Mega Junko, Sosho Shukyo ni Okeru Joseikyoso no Boseikan, in Bosei wo Tou (ge) ed. Wakita Haruko, Jinbun Shoin, Kyoto, 1988.

[27] Ibid.

saviours, Bunjiro's views cannot be recognised as having surmounted the traditional male perspective on women.

The background to Miki, Kino and Nao's awareness of possessing elements of both female and male sexuality was, as Mega Junko has pointed out, the influence of society in an era in which the constraints of mens domination over women was strongly reflected, and in order for these women founders and their teachings to be accepted they had to supplement their selves with masculine elements. Tadano Makuzu, the pioneer of the concept of modern womens liberation, was also judged as a woman possessing a man's spirit. But in the case of these three women founders of religions it is significant that they themselves came up with a model for the total liberation of both men and women through the coexistence of both genders in their personalities.

Such popular religious sects (with the exception of Nyoraikyo), staked their destiny during the formation of the Meiji era on adhering to the values of the Emperor system by reforming and reorganising as Sect Shinto. Amidst strained relations with State Shinto as organisation under central administration proceeded, the sects which were originally built upon the innovativeness of their women founders, also gradually became more conservative and began to internalise the same kind of sexual discrimination as established religions. Even in Tenrikyo the 'theory of male and female cooperation' that Miki preached became fixed as a theory of distinct sexual roles to promote the ideal of a 'good wife and wise mother' advocated in the Imperial Message on Education.[28] This tendency to adopt a position of complementing the Emperor system became a marked characteristic of the various new religions that developed and became accepted after the second world war (with the exception of the Honmichi sect which faithfully restored the spirit of Nakayama Miki and tried to liberate themselves from the spell of the Emperor system).

In the headstream of modern new religions descended from the Hokke sect (also known as the Nichiren or Lotus sect), is one called

---

[28] Usui Atsuko, Shinshukyo to Josei, in Shukyo Shakaigaku Kenkyukai, Ima Shukyo wo Dou Toraeruka, Kaimeisha, Tokyo, 1992.

Reiyukai. Reiyukai has a particular fascination for housewives because of the veneration it preaches for ancestors of both spouses. Normally a married woman is no longer regarded as a member of the *ie* in which she was born, and must worship only the ancestors of her *ie* by marriage. Reiyukai encouraged the worship of women's blood ancestors, and in doing so went beyond the traditional view of direct ancestral lineage reinforcing the patriarchal family structure, to open up a completely new world of meaning for women cut off from worship of their blood ancestors. Nevertheless Kotani Kimi, the leader of Reiyukai who bestowed this right on her female followers, also preached 'a change of heart' as a means of solving familial problems and reaffirmed the traditional social division of roles that dictates a woman stays inside the home and the man goes out, and a wife should follow the lead set by her husband. Kimi also did not approve of both spouses working.

Tracing the historical development and structure of new religions in this way reveals the similarities to the traditional state religions of Buddhism and Shinto. Soka Gakkai and Rissho Koseikai, a large group descended from the Nichiren sect, are typical examples of this. Koiseikai was formed by a female shaman, Naganuma Myoko, and a male cofounder, Niwano Nikkyo, who took charge of doctrine and rules. During the early stages of the group, seven out of eight secretariat leaders were women, however following the death of Naganuma after the war the importance of teaching was strongly advocated and energy poured into the establishment of doctrine and development of organisational structure. At present the backbone of the group is comprised of men, and a distinct principle of gender role discrimination dominates in the way that men maintain the bureaucratic organisation while women carry out the menial daily tasks.

Despite the innovative views of these women founders who preached traditional division of roles according to gender, with man as chief and woman as subordinate, were a common characteristic of new religions. The domestic role upheld for women in Soka Gakkai, for example, is grounded in the Nichiren teaching that "a woman while obeying all is obeyed by all" (see chapter by Haga Akira). Except in special cases where the husband opposes the wife's faith, all women were taught the moral value of 'subordination' as expounded in the *Jokunsho*. Another new religion, Jissen Rinri Koseikai, compares the husband to an 'active' locomotive pulling his wife the 'passive' passenger car, along behind. Women are taught to become an attractive wife rather than a clever one. The publications of religious groups give many examples of discordant, stormy households being returned to peace through these principles being put into practice.

Not only the religions mentioned so far, but other religions with many women followers such as Myochikai and Nenposhinkyo, teach women to 'step back' and defer to others. Following traditional Japanese values, new religious groups preached the sacred worth of the *ie* and the division of roles according to gender. Through successfully stepping back and observing such divisions, order and peace in the 'sacred' *ie* are restored and housewives freed from their 'unhappy' situation. This kind of peace may seem suspect in the eyes of a third party, but in the subjective consciousness of the person concerned, the unhappiness is dissolved.

On the whole, new religions teach that poverty, sickness, conflict and various other social anomalies, including sexual discrimination, are situations that can be defrayed through changing one's attitude, thus transforming them into internal problems. The great effectiveness of new religions' teaching that "to change another person you must first change yourself. The other person will change as a result," has been pointed out in Hamaguchi Keishun's proposal of a Japanese society which has the distinguishing characteristic of a 'human principle' (ie. social value in which smooth human relations are achieved through mutual dependance of self and other).[29] Not only new religions, but all religions differ from an ideology pressing for social reform, in that they hold the key to changing ones world view itself. Both Christianity and Buddhism are quite clear on this point.

---

[29] Numata Kenya, Gendai Nihon no Shinshukyo, Sogensha, Osaka, 1988. Also see chapter by Igeta Midori.

However in a true religious community, when faced with such absolute holy values as those of a transcendent deity or the nothingness of Nirvana, worldly values are sublated and the world of a new system of values opens up. A subjective change of heart can be very attractive when faced with this new world of values.

And what of new religions? Almost all religious groups are the same; by the very affirmation and acceptance of the wordly value system itself that includes relations between the rulers (the strong) and the ruled (the weak), there is no intention to sublate. In the world of new religions, the strong remaining strong and the weak remaining weak is not thought unjust. The strong are influenced by the dynamics of the weak deferring, or the weak believe that in the cyclical theory of transmigration (ie. in this life a former life or the next), they will recieve the status of the strong and that in the end everyone is equal. Or, there is the schemata in which not only a murderer, but also the victim is apportioned responsibility for a crime. For example, women who are molested are not accepted as pure victims because it is said that 'she wasn't on her guard.' If this logic is extended there is the danger that it will be coupled directly with the absurd argument that the socially weak, including women, must be resigned to their status as weak on account of their own guilt. The weak have the same human rights as the strong, and in a society which lacks a world view in which everything is relativised by a commonly understood metaphysical principle, the victims of discrimination do not receive genuine justice, and anger and sadness are temporarily numbed by a change of heart - which is nothing more than false comfort. In a 'human principle' society, genuine social equality connoting also the weak is not encouraged.

Finally, I would like to look at the teachings of new religions on the 'sacred' division of roles by gender, which modern men and women must fill. Corresponding to men's role as promoters of industry leading to national prosperity, is a schemata of women's role being to take care of the spirits of ancestors and aborted children, raise children and care for aged parents, which all amounts to tranquility in the *ie*. This line coincides exactly with the social welfare policy of the Liberal

Democratic Party. Many sects continue to preach that the symptoms born of the strains of modern education, such as children who refuse to attend school and various other unhappinesses that befall the home, are due to the curses of ancestors or aborted children. And for immature youth who do not have the confidence to select their own marriage partner, groups such as the Unification Church are happy to act as go-betweens or consultants in the same way as they do for taking exams, and basically function in such a way as to compensate for the fundamental poverty of education and welfare policies of present government.

Even if the teachings of various religious groups do seem suspect, housewives who have regained tranquility in their home and spirit through these teachings and their religious activities, have fulfilled one kind of desire for power, not only in the home but in society as well, and can live personally fulfilled lives (see Igeta Midori's chapter). Looking at the statistics, women are more active as teachers and believers in new religions than traditional ones. Their activities are an alibi concealing the various absurdities of new religions, the unilateral pushing of sexual discrimination in the division of roles by gender, and the poverty of Japanese politics.

Women and Nation - Reflections on the *Kojiki*

Kono Nobuko

1. The Female Principle

Pioneering feminist and historian, Takamure Itsue, began her research in women's history by attempting to comprehend Motoori Norinaga's detailed study of the Shinto classic, *Kojiki den*. The reason for this, she wrote, was because "from early on I was heedful of the National Learning[1] scholars' conception of women's history." But anarchist trends in Japanese intellectual circles of the time, however, could also not be disregarded, as Takamure and her husband, Hashimoto Kenzo, had close connections to the anarchist movement. And, they were also on close terms with Ishikawa Sanshiro, who published *Kojiki Shinwa no Shinkenkyu* (New Research on Mythology of the *Kojiki*) in 1921. This book was ignored in academic circles, but nevertheless became a longseller with the 13th edition published in 1933.

Towards the end of the Taisho period (1912-26) a period of radicalism in intellectual circles drew to a close, but the surge of interest in the *Kojiki* from that time continued well into the following Showa period. There was another surge of interest in the *Kojiki*, which I too was drawn into, directly after the wave of opposition to the United States-Japan Security Treaty of 1960.

The anarchist Ishikawa Sanshiro stated during the Taisho period that "the state is a common illusion," and the radical poet Yoshimoto Takaaki reiterated this after the 1960 Japan-U.S. Security Treaty. At this time the trend was to read the *Kojiki* as a means of searching for

---

[1] National Learning was a general name for the textual and interpretative study of Japanese classical literature. It was the basis for creating a new concept of nation by scholars active in the imperial restoration movement, and was also used by some nationalist zealots as an ideological framework for the imperial Japanese state in the years before World War II. Translator's note.

clues to the depths of popular consciousness of this enveloping "common illusion."

There was also the somewhat vain hope, that details of the past would provide explanations for current states of affairs. So it was that women of those times found themselves with the task of searching for distortions and blurring of the female principle in the *Kojiki*, and its subsequent distortions.

2. *Spoken and Written*

The style of language used in the *Kojiki* is difficult to ascribe as the work of a woman. O no Yasumaro himself, the scholar-official who transcribed it in the 8th century, stated that the expression had been changed into a written form.

In ancient times it was difficult to subdue both word and meaning to construct a sentence and turn it into script. The writing system at the time depended on the usage of Chinese characters, which were used as simply phonetic symbols to represent native Japanese words, or could be used as ideographs to represent meaning and were pronounced in Japanese to reflect the original Chinese pronounciation. If stated in *kun*, that is as a native Japanese word, the written meaning did not coincide with the meaning of the word as spoken, and if connected entirely phonetically then the narrative became very long.[2]

The narrator of the *Kojiki* was a blind oral historian called Hieda no Are, sex unknown, who recited the imperial genealogy and legends which O no Yasumaro transcribed. If this person were a woman, then the oral textual subdivisions would have disappeared at the time of transcription.

Kataribe were hereditary occupational group specialising in reciting orally transmitted texts at court ceremonies in ancient times. Hieda no Are was a member of a *kataribe*, and must be seen as a

---

[2] Preface by Kurano Kenji to annotated Kojiki, pp. 16-17, Iwanami Shoten, Tokyo, 1963. The following quotations from the Kojiki are from the same source.

functionary representative of the group, not as an individual.[3] The basis for inferring that the *kataribe* were composed of women, is expounded by Yanagita Kunio in his book *Hieda no Are*:

The makeup and selection of material for the *Kojiki* lead if anything to the supposition that it was the work of one intelligent, female oral historian. For example many beautiful *uta monogatari* [tales formed around poems], interesting stories of the origins of proverbs and poems are central, and public and private trifling matters are frequently recollected, while pressing matters of importance such as transitions in government are sometimes disregarded ...[4]

Yanagita also closely examines the formation of Hieda no Are's clan and its lineage. It is irrational, however, to assume that the narrator is a woman because there are "many beautiful *uta monogatari*." Such an assumption would necessitate determining other facts such as whether or not there was succession through the maternal line within the group. But this is a debate into which I do not want to enter into any further here.

The language culture already existant at the time the ancient nation was forming, had a vitality and power to stir, and there was an apparent hestitation to suppress this by the imposition of a foreign script, in this case Chinese characters. Consequently the intermediation of Hieda no Are's oral transmission, completely free from the restraints of written language, would have been unavoidable.

At this stage the male principle had not become dominant, and male and female were still regarded on an equal footing. There is a scene in the the first volume of the *Kojiki* where the spiritual, material and physical power of the female principle is vividly described with expressions more beautiful than others used elsewhere. Supposing that Hieda no Are were a man, even if these 'feminine parts' were not substituted with 'maternal parts,' the male perspective could still survive.

---

[3] Such narrators were referred to as 'servants' and vacancies were filled with members of the same family as Hieda no Are. Refer to Yanagita Kunio's work Hieda no Are regarding this.

[4] Yanagita Kunio, Imoto no Chikara, p. 290, Kadokawa Shoten, Tokyo 1971.

3. The Force of Fire and Blood

The female deity, Izanami, died giving birth to the fire deity. Her husband, Izanagi, then crawled and wept at her pillow and her feet, like a female mourner. An ethnologist might suppose that in those times, when a wife died men had to crawl around weeping as a kind of rite, but as we cannot be certain of the truth we are left only with the fact of the ancient acceptance of a man crying, be it as part of a ritual or arising from a well of emotion.

From the first, legends have arisen around the world concerning man's sense of culpability in obtaining fire; the illusion of Prometheus, the myth of Caldea, even in modern day Japan the fire god is treated as a guardian deity with great miracle working power. Many taboos arose around this guardian deity. The myth of Izanami dying after giving birth to the fire god can also be categorised as complex, however the corpse of Izanami was also the source of various physical images and images of birth in the common consciousness of the ancients, through the other deities which are born out of Izanami's excreta and vomit as she dies: the male and female metal deities, Kanayama Hiko and Kanayama Hime; male and female earth deities, Haniyasu Hiko and Haniyasu Hime; the female water deity, Mitsuhanome; the male production deity, Wakumusuhi; and a female deity controlling food, Toyoke Hime. Originally the fire deity Izanami gave birth to had a triple-barrel name, Hinoyagihayao Hinokagahiko Hinokagutsuchi, which signified light, power and fragrance.

In the age in which the *Kojiki* was written there was no sense of death as a defilement or impure. If anything, the narrative shows that originally death was not regarded as an impure phenomenon, but at the point where the gods' descendants descend to earth, the concept of impurity appears in conjunction with the death of Amenowakahiko. It is still a matter of dispute, however, as to whether the modern character meaning "impurity" is accurate or not, and there are homonymous phrases with different characters which could also be interpreted as the original meanings. For example, phrases meaning "the commonplace is exhausted" and "the spirit is extended (meaning supernatural spiritual power)," were also possible interpretations of the word which now has 'impurity' as its designated meaning.

Izanagi's 'weeping woman' behaviour exemplifies an 'extension of the spirit' in many opinions, and his tears instantly give rise to a spring. Next is the appearance of blood; Izanagi cuts the neck of the fire deity, Gagutsuchi, who caused his wife's death, and "the blood that stained the sword splashed on a cluster of holy rocks, and became the deity named Iwasaku .... ."

Language in this section of the *Kojiki* is suggestive of the forceful power of 'dynamic blood.' Images of the deities Iwasaku and Nesaku are consistent with physical images of electrical phenomenon and powerful magma at the beginning of life on earth. Then there is also Iwatsutsunoo, who dwells in the rocks, and Mikahayahi and Hihayahi who evoke the sun. Takemikazuchi is synonymous with thunder. They are all the original source of running blood.

Today this scenario does not apply because we cannot turn back time to know what happened before the birth of the solar system. However, the creation of the solar system can be given a parallel counterpart through creating physical images of the origin of blood in the gods. The French philosopher Simone Weil, is said to have called the god who killed the fire deity, and the soul of the people who submit to that god, the "mutual madness of god and man."

Today we still do not know if women could create this grand design of bloodlines. There have been various attempts, however, to debate the subject from the perspective of womens's history.

4. Non-possession of Blood

The feminist historian Barbara Duden said of women's bodies that "there is always a divided understanding," and "it has been considered natural that women have always been prone to pregnancy, menstruation and menopause," but poses the question of whether this is really so.[5] The 'body theory' methodology in women's history research, and "knowing how women came historically to acquire their bodies, is a central concern of women's history" which springs from this question.

The source of Duden's research was the records kept by an early 18th century German doctor living in Eisenhauer. For 20 years this doctor kept records covering several thousand pages, of 1,700 womens comments and feelings about their bodies and internal parts. The results showed that "not one of these women regarded their body as their own possession" and Duden reaches the conclusion that "unlike today, women of 200 years ago did not think of their bodies and its internal parts in terms of the concept of possession at all." It was more than a hundred years since William Harvey had advanced the theory of blood circulation, yet there was still no sense of ownership of blood. Duden found this difficult to understand.

The analytical thinking of modern medicine has implanted in people a concept of body ownership, but today there is again an increasing tendency for people to feel that they do not own the inside of their bodies. As Duden points out, modern medicine is based on a discontinuity of early 18th century medicine's perceptions of women's bodies, and contemporary perceptions. Today, however, many women are becoming aware of the subtler issues regarding their bodies; for them there is no doubt that an individual is the proprietor of the body's internal parts. Under this custodianship, any outsiders who venture there, whether it be as spirit, god, or in biological form, are only temporary residents. This was a new concept of blood and the body.

The ability to regard oneself in such detail, however, is a double-edged sword; on the one hand people set themselves free by seeing the individual as a 'lump of flesh' and 'owner of internal organs,' on the other they possess an evil spirit quite capable of violating the spirit of rules and regulations, by seeing the body as distinct from the personality. Hence there are many obstacles to overcome for people

---

[5] Barbara Duden, Maruoka Hideoka to no Taidan - Josei no Shintai to Seikatsu no Rekishi, interpreted by Ito Ruri, hosted by Nagahata Michiko, in Jenda-, Moji, Shintai, Shin Hyoron, Tokyo, 1986.

seeking to escape these restrictions, and in the methods of women's history.

Barbara Duden's first reaction to the book by Ivan Illich, H_2O and the Waters of Forgetfulness, was "why has he not described blood?"[6] In this book there is a particular adherence to a time sequential history of material substance. Illich says for example, "The substance thought of as 'water' or 'fire' differs according to the culture and the age. Water is also always dualistic." Even the boundary between fire and water is not a rigid one, and "it can be said of whichever tribe we are speaking of, that beneath the numerous images we form of water in our imaginations, expressions, moods, sensory experiences and light, there is a substance praised which is like tranquil, strong, flowing water, and which is secretly growing amongst us."[7] The flow of space and time examined in the light and sound of water, is developed based on the work of French philosopher, Gaston Bachelard. But as Barbara Duden points out, blood is used as a metaphor even though there is no apparent mention of it as the foundation.

Differences emerge in the 'common illusion' spoken of by Ishikawa Sanshiro and Yoshimoto Takaaki, according to whether a tribe believes their origins to be in the sea or the mountains. Tribes who believe in the powerful effects of blood, tend to regard the sea as their origin in myths of creation. In the *Kojiki*, the sea is the beginning; "the sea water was churned up and rumbled, and when the spear was lifted, brine trickled down from the tip." After the islands are born from the drops which trickled down, the gods of the sea, rivers, streams and watersheds are born. This is the reverse of the upstream, midstream and downstream order that modern people imagine.

Today there is a tendency for water to be thought of in conjunction with purification. Even politicians use the word in reference to atonement for their offences. Cleansing in sea water remains a part of festival activities, reflecting an illusion of ancient times, but otherwise

---

6   Statement at Waseda Hoshien, December 1986.
7   Ivan Illich, H_2O to Mizu, transl. Ito Ruri, Tokyo, 1986 (H_2O and the Waters of Forgetfulness, Boyars, London, 1986).

continues to die out in daily life. Indeed it may be possible to 'go to the river to wash,' but there is no equivalent expression 'go to the sea to wash.' Blood, one other aspect of the sea route, is something that has to be washed away if it flows outside a traveller's body, and no longer has any symbolism or magical power.

This represents one kind of liberation, but in the original thinking of tribes who gave power to the existence of blood through the medium of fire, the more there was an artificial separation of water and H_2O, the more people's thoughts became fragmented, resulting in the degradation of 'blood and impurity,' and leaving only discrimination. Barbara Duden maintains that not all tribes were so, because there are also tribes with creation myths starting from the sea and moving to blood.

The brilliance of water is 'pure and beautiful,' but this is a distorted view, for water that descends from the mountains is filtered.

The world which gave birth to the illusion that fire is the medium between the sea and blood, is also the place which created the twofold existence of 'red' and 'black.'

5. Concept of Life

In the beginning, the *Kojiki* depicts death and darkness as a feast of electrical phenomenon which are the origins of life, but this perception gradually changes and there is a shift toward the notion of the impurity of death when the passage on Amenowakahiko is reached.

It is difficult to know whether or not the narrators of the *Kojiki* regretted the disappearance of this notion of darkness as the pivotal point of the cosmos, a development which occurred during the process of formation of the state. According to how it is read, the *Kojiki* can also be taken as a book showing the decline of a concept of life.

A rumbling swarm of maggots, with a great thunderbolt at the head, lightning in the chest, black thunderbolt in the belly, forked lightning in the shadow, young lightning in the left hand, earth lightning in the right hand, thunder in the left foot, sheet lightning

in the right foot, altogether eight pillars of lightning deities
(Passage on land of the dead)[8]

This view of life and death changes when it comes to the passage
on Amenowakahiko. Takamimusuhi and Amaterasu receive the assent
of the council of eight million deities to send Amenohohino from
heaven to negotiate with Okuninushi about yielding the land, but after
three years of currrying favour with Okuninushi, Amenohohino had
not brought back any reply, and so Amenowakahiko was sent.
Amenowakahiko, however, married Shitateruhime, the daughter of
Okuninushi, and still did not return after eight years. Next Nakime (a
pheasant) went to urge things on but was shot by Amenowakahiko in a
commotion. The arrow that killed her was shot back by Takamimusuhi
and Amenowakahiko died. A friend who was said to resemble
Amenowakahiko and came to the funeral, became angry and kicked
down the funeral house in protest, saying "What are you talking about!
Comparing me to a filthy corpse!"

The attitude of the friend, Ajishikitakahikone, is quite different to
Izanagi's, who had visited the land of the dead. The corpse of
Amenowakahiko also differs from Izananmi's in not being a display of
thunder and lightening.

Blood was originally viewed as the origin of life and the gods, but
at some point this perception changed and it came to be seen as
polluting. The state established a common illusion by implanting the
notion of impurity as black impurity (death), and red impurity
(women's blood). This also became linked to a philosophy of cosmic
principle (concept of deities) opposing purity and impurity.

Despite this separation in ancient times, the consciousness of the
sea as an origin has become interwoven with that of water and blood,
and survived to modern times, latent in people's consciousnesses. For
example, during the Meiji era Izumi Kyoka resurrected *Koya Hijiri*[9]
(The Itinerant Monk) in a bedevillment of water and blood. In *Koya
Hijiri*, leeches appear as the cause of destruction of the world.

---

8 Kojiki, pp. 26 - 27, Iwanami Shoten, Tokyo, 1963.
9 In Gendai Bungaku Taikei, vol. 2, p. 60, Chikuma Shobo, Tokyo, 1965.

Since mythical times incomparably fearful leeches had camped here, moving around and waiting for people to happen by. When after a long time they had taken their fill of blood and satiated their desires, the leeches vomited up all the blood, causing the earth to liquify and the forest to change into a swamp of blood and mud. At the same time the sun was blocked, it became dark, and one by one the large trees turned into leeches. What a thing, it truly was.

Koya Hijiri appears at this point, disregarding the Revelation of St. John, he says that even if the destruction of this world is "not the earths cover breaking, fire raining down from the sky, and oceans covering the earth," we were shown a vision of the mountains and earth caving in through the disgorging of the blood swallowed by the leeches.

In the *Kojiki*, Izanami was not an agent of this kind of devilish chaos, but as the deity who gave birth to the sun and fire he epitomises lightning and demonstrates clearly an existence aboveground. The aboveground sun and underground lightning are linked in the narration.

Izanagi shows no spirit and simply runs away. If Izanami is the symbol of the rule of lightning and fire, humans would not be able to bring their pleas for mercy to her if they were on an equal level. The narrator of the *Kojiki* states that escape was possible by simply running away. There is also the theory that Izanagi's running around and brandishing a sword, is a kind of purification spell taken from Taoism.[10] It is also apparent from the preface to the *Kojiki* that from the end of the 7th century through the eighth century, the *bunshohakushi* (scribes) may have become independent of the *kataribe*, and inserted Taoist elements in places. Scribes were a more likely means of keeping records than folk stories, folklore and *fudoki*, the provincial gazettes with reports of natural resources, geophysical conditions and oral traditions of each region. If the Emperor had Taoist leanings then it would be even more likely. Nevertheless, I would like to refrain from picking out the insertion of Taoist, Confucianist and Buddhist ideas into the *Kojiki*. Even if the Emperor

---

[10] Chusei shin, Kojiki wo Yomu, Kadokawa Shoten, Tokyo, 1985.

and the scribes did have Taoist leanings, the nation's politics could not very well continue forever without changing the notion of the state to one which reflected the structure and cosmic principle of the world. In due time there was a shift in focus from a common illusion to a concept, which inevitably became discussed as a principle of administration. The beginnings of this process appear directly in the *Kojiki*.

6. The Disappearance of Reading the Moon and Stars

The subject of government and rule is gradually introduced in the *Kojiki* from the birth of Amaterasu onwards. Izanami, the progenitor, was responsible for not only the universal principle itself, but also light and the gravity of darkness, and divided the important tasks of ruling the country between Amaterasu, Tsukuyomi and Susanoo.

Such a division of power could possibly be explained by referring to the *fudoki* for each region and the various tales of tribal conflict and alliances recorded there. But this would only be speculation, for all we have left is a narrative contaning a vision of a united country, one in which Izanami has been distanced from the position of Great Mother God, and the will of the tribal alliance which places Amaterasu as the great Mother God, prevails.

For some reason Tsukuyomi, the person who reads the moon, disappears in the process and appears no more in the narrative. What kind of phenomenon could Tsukuyomi's physical image be based on that he is only mentioned once?

In the main body of the *Kojiki*, the characters used for Tsukuyomi are those for 'moon'- *tsku*, and 'read' - *yomi*. The diversity of meanings possible from a phonetic rendition become limited when Chinese characters are used, putting greater stress on the original concept. O no Yasumaro demonstrated his power to expunge in the act of transcribing the narration. The name Tsukuyomi, which was at first written with the character for *yomi* meaning Land of the Dead, was not developed in the narrative and became *yomi* meaning 'read' in later passages. If written this way, it could have disappeared because later generations, people who read 'Tsukuyomi' to mean the moon, did not have roots in the myths of this country or tribal alliances of the time.

Taking into consideration a later calendar of the province, it is clear that people followed the phases of the moon, as changes of the tides were deeply connected to survival of the race. They would not have thought much of Tsukuyomi's disappearance then, because the moon was not mysterious, but simply a natural phenomenon understood by them. For the ruling powers and authorities also, the moon was a predictable element which did not cause internal opposition and conflict. Like the ocean, Susanoo's realm, the moon does not play tricks. The moon and its effect, became, if anything, merged with the ocean:

> In the 384,400 kilometre circle drawn in empty space by heaven's unseen meridians sitting astride the skies, when the moon is passing with an angular velocity of 14 degrees thirty minutes per hour, its gravitational pull affects most strongly the earth your foot is treading on now.

> If the surface your foot were treading on at that moment were the sea, surrounding water would flow towards that point and before long it would fill up and overflow, and eventually you would be standing straight in the wide brimming surface of the tide.[11]

There is no difference in principle between modern natural science and the combined intuition and experience from the era of the *Kojiki*. Consequently Kinoshita Junji could produce a work based on the tale of the last sea battle of the Heike family, in which there is a harmonising of the meridian, the moon and the sea in the opening and closing passages. This was also a passage narrated at the opening and closing of the first stage performance in 1978.

Naturally there is also much about sea routes in the *Kojiki*; *Kamuyamatoiharehiko* (Emperor Jimmu) resembles the *Heike Monogatari* (The Tale of the Heike) in using the Inland Sea as a sea route. The pilot is the local earth god who knows the sea routes well.

---

[11] Kinoshita Junji, Shigosen no Matsuri, p. 6, Kawade Bunko, Tokyo, 1990.

At some stage the north star came to play a more important role than either the moon or sun in determining bearings with the naked eye on land and at sea. But despite this, reading the stars is not mentioned in the *Kojiki*. It suggests that the diversification and confusion of theories surrounding origins of the Japanese race may be connected with the disappearance of reading the stars from the *Kojiki*. Contradictions emerge if it is believed that in the process of writing the *Kojiki* the *kataribe* did not pass on any information about the stars. It also cannot be supposed that the tribes of the different regions were uninterested in the stars.

In China and India the ecliptic degrees of the system of astrology based on zodiacal constellations and known in Japanese as *nijuhachishuku,* were developed in approximately 1000 BC. This system is still used for forecasting good and bad luck in shrine calendars. The importance of astrology is also reflected in Emperor Temmu's (?-686) penchant for it in the construction of Ise Shrine, as ethnologist Yoshino Hiroko has also pointed out.

Stars were used as a guide to the agricultural seasons amongst the general populace. The Pleiades rising in the east in June, indicated the time of rice planting. The North star, particularly important to fishermen, was called the Myoken star in Shimane and Oita prefectures and the Uminari star in Iwate prefecture. Southern tribes which came to Japan along the sea routes, had probably already established reading of the stars. It is also known that names were given to the stars in Utaki in the islands of Okinawa.

It is doubtful whether the Tanabata Festival in Japan was originally a star festival, but in folk custom, water deity festivals merged with star festivals. At the very least in the area around Yamato (Nara prefecture), it seems that a romantic story was attached to the brightest stars in the harp and eagle constellations. Within Taoism there were also rites for the purification of 'evil' stars, as comets were regarded as an ill-omen in ancient Japan.

There may have been no reading of the stars in the *Kojiki*, but when Amaterasu welcomes Susanoo to the heavens she wears in her hair shining jewels reminiscent of the Pleiades. The constellation of

Pleiades has six individual stars visible to the naked eye, which would have seemed like six individual balls grouped together. The Pleiades were also a symbol of both good and ill fortune. There was a proverb amongst farmers of the country which said that if buckwheat seed were sowed when the Pleiades were directly overhead, the harvest would be plentiful. Since ancient times shrine calendars have closely followed the cycle of seasons and production, and according to the *nihachiyado*, Pleiades signified "a very lucky day, good for everything" in the Fukuoka shrine calendar, and "favorable for supplying horses and cows, wearing *hakama* (traditional clothing), digging wells, but unlucky for cutting out and making things" in the Tokyo shrine calendar. There is a clear difference of opinion between the Tokyo and Fukuoka shrines regarding reading of the stars; for example the Fukuoka almanac says of the constellation which is the western part of Aquarius, that it is a "very unlucky day, everything will turn out badly," while the Tokyo almanac has "good for studying the performing arts, good for wearing new things, unfavourable for holding funerals."

These examples alone of reading the stars, illustrate how the extinction of tradition was a function of changes according to the authority, and the *nijuhachishuku*, originally a means of partitioning in the astronomical theory of existence, became linked to the forces of fortune through the corruption of natural science. But people continue to seek their fortunes in the stars because astrology and natural science are entangled in their minds.

7. *Festivals of Blood and The Power of Darkness*

Death was the 'black impurity' which caused the 'red impurity,' however, in time the 'power of darkness' was shown to be not only a magical but a physical power as well. One person to do this was Miyazawa Kenji, speaking through a fantasy story:

Jobani looked there and was quite startled. In one part of the Milky Way an enormous deep black hole had opened up. However much he strained his eyes it was not possible to see how deep the bottom was or if there were something inside - his eyes merely hurt even more.[12]

This corresponds to the black hole next to the southern cross in the central part of the Milky Way Galaxy. The powerful electromagnetic waves emanating from this black hole have been verified.

The section in the *Kojiki* concerning Izanami and the murdered fire deity is identified as the origin from which a powerful mass of death, darkness and blood emanates, yet this principle later disappears from the sequence of events. Mythologists have identified from this chronicle, the people who created tales of not only the birth of the country but also the cosmic genesis, and shifts in development of similar races have also been traced. Mapping of the generation of mythological legends, however, is best left to the respective scholars. All that remains now, is like an entangled mass of fine roots in the earth, with the origins of none very clear.

The next occurrence of a large river of blood appears in connection with the myth of Susanoo and Yamata no Orochi, the eight-headed, eight-tailed snakelike monster. "The monster was cut and scattered into many pieces, and the water of the river Hino flowed with blood,"[13] is a description strikingly like a lava flow.

The only place where the *Kojiki* evolves any grand design of blood and death is in the section concerning Izanami of the Land of the Dead and Yamata no Orochi. Hieda no Are, (the group and the individual) possibly wanted only to relate the thoughts of the gods in heaven. Phrases used in this section such as *orochi* (big snake) are not apparent in later sections:

Those eyes were red, and on one body there were eight heads and eight tails. Moss and cryptomerias grew out of the body, and its length stretched along eight vallies in which its tails lay, and blood could be seen continually flowing from the stomach.[14]

---

[12] Miyazawa Kenji, Ginga Tetsudo no Yoru, p. 124, Shinko Bunko, Tokyo, 1961.
[13] Kojiki, p. 40, Iwanami Shoten, Tokyo, 1963.
[14] Ibid. p. 39.

In the structure of control formed by the state, death is usually impure and the consciousness of blood as impure found its way into the sequence. This was accompanied by ritualisation of ceremonies to calm the dead, because rampaging of souls of the dead would bring trouble. Accordingly, women as well as men accepted this notion for a long time. As might be expected, this section continues to predict the distortions in men's and women's memories, and can be thought of as a message woven into the narration.

Blood and death, like the origins of physical and spiritual power, run throughout the myths of the *Kojiki*. Yet if blood is the food of the sun, there are aspects in which it might become like an Aztec blood ceremony, even in the minds of people with the same beliefs in a sun god.

In his book *Kokubo to Kokukshin, Momotaro no Haha* (Cereal Mother and Cereal Deity, Momotaro's Mother),[15] Ishida Eiichiro refers to the writings of a sixteenth century Spanish priest about the festival of Teteoinnan. This is a festival held for the female deity Teteoinnan and for the corn harvest in November. Even the following simple summary conveys the impression of a group illusion with a bloody conclusion.

A woman from forty to forty five years old was chosen as the goddess, Teteoinnan. More a sacrifice than a goddess, she was attired in beautiful clothes. A female shaman then conducted a mock battle for four days, after which time the goddess was taken to the temple and beheaded by a priest. Next a tall strong priest dressed in the skin of her body. By donning this skin the priest becomes Teteoinnan. Proceeding to other temples, he is welcomed by soldiers bearing blood-stained brooms who, while fighting, accompany him to the temple of the sun god. The next day is for sacrificing prisoners. First 'she' (the priest wearing the skin of the slain goddess is referred to as female) kills four prisoners, and taking out the hearts, offers them to the gods. The remaining prisoners are killed by other priests.

---

[15] Kodansha, Tokyo, 1972.

The light of the sun is necessary in order to harvest the corn. Yet the sun goes to sleep everyday and loses vigor as winter approaches. These people could not conceive of an immutable sun, and so they thought that the blood of humans must be drunk to strengthen the weakening sun.

Apart from the woman chosen as the goddess, they also drank the blood of slaves. Priests substituted the blood of slaves when they were supposed to offer their own. It seems that in the period up to the sixteenth century, priests in this region had worked out a very convenient method to conduct the festival through the blood of others. It could also be thought of as a culture which had not yet arrived at substituting blood with wine, flesh with bread, and real people with dolls.

In the *Kojiki*, Izanami was distanced from the position of the Great Mother ancestral deity, and Amaterasu brought to the fore as the Sun deity, and so the concept of human blood as food of the sun did not remain. But from this we cannot jump to the conclusion that only tribes who did not once conduct blood festivals inhabited the Japanese archipelago.

The line, "Originally I had eight daughters but every year the Yamata no Orochi comes to eat them"[16] has something about it evocative of a 'blood festival.' The phrase "the river Hino flowed with blood" consequently bears further investigation for concealed meaning. While mythologists and ethnologists have various interpretations for this "flow of blood" and eating of "eight maidens," natural scientists also have quite feasible explanations connecting it to the natural world.

In the *Nihon Shoki*,[17] there is an emphatic disavowal of the concept of *junshi* (self-immolation on the death of one's master) in the passage on the Emperor Suijin from Volume 6.[18]

---

[16] Kojiki, p.39, Iwanami Shoten, Tokyo, 1963.

[17] From No. 67 of Nihon Koten Bungaku Taikei, Iwanami Shoten, Tokyo, 1967.

[18] Emperor Suijin, otherwise known as Ikumeiribiko was at least the eleventh generation, but there is no actual proof of existence, however there is also no reason to dismiss it as merely myth. In the Nihon Rekishi Gakkai, Nihonshi

On the death of the Empress Hibasuhime, the Emperor asked his retainers whether "the practice of following a master by committing suicide on the death of a member of the nobility" was a good one or not. At this one of the senior statesmen, Nomi no Sukune, came forward and said "burying living people in the Emperor's tomb is not good. Please wait while I try to think of some solution." He sent a messenger to the Hajibe (the group in charge of funerals and making haniwa) in Izumo (now Shimane prefecture) and presented to the Emperor clay figurines of various shapes including horses and humans, with the proposal that "in future these figures made of clay will be placed in the tomb as a substitute for humans, and I would like this to be a rule for generations to come." The Emperor was greatly pleased, saying to Nomi no Sukune, "I grant your proposal from my heart" and gave the command, "from now on these clay figures will be placed in the tomb and people must not harmed." Through this Nomi no Sukune became founder of the Hajibe, the guild in charge of funerals and making the clay figures.[19] Therefore it is believed that up until this time the practice of burying people alive, did exist.

In the folklore of each region there were also tales of human sacrifice such as Matsuo Kenji and Sayo Hime. There is something similar, difficult to say exactly what, in these legends of human sacrifice, which spread throughout the country somehow, becoming localised legends in each region in a form 'showing spiritual power and worshipped as gods.'

The practice of following a master's death by committing suicide ceased in the course of forming the ancient state. This practice cannot be taken as simply fiction because it is written in the *Gishiwajinden* (The Wei Chronicles), "When Himiko died, a large tumulus was made. The diameter was over one hundred steps, and over a hundred male and female servants were buried with her." The narration of the *Kojiki* is not as direct as the *Nihon Shoki* on this point. Where does this lack of directness come from I wonder?

Nenpyo, Iwanami Shoten, Tokyo, 1966, the Emperor's reign period first appears from the 26th generation Emperor Keitai in the year 507.

[19] In the Kojiki this point is put exceedingly simply as "Hajibe was established."

I would like to close with the following conclusions:
1. The narrator had no interest in the practice of *junshi*.
2. The second volume does not have the scope for natural spirits to flow as freely through it as in the first volume, and was not considererd by the *kataribe* to be their work.
3. As the state took shape, there was no margin for associating with disturbing female deities, and the *Kojiki* was the last work of the guild known as the *kataribe*, which disappeared to be replaced by the *hajibe* and *ishiku* (stonemasons) guilds. Records of the Emperor's reign period etc were not entrusted to the *kataribe*, but were ranked as official written court records.

Through such a state of affairs, the *kataribe*, who held a vision of the power of darkness, became *arukimiko* (women capable of transmitting through trance the utterance of a supernatural being, or walking females in service of shrines), travelling through the country and telling their tales, which became transformed into local 'legends of human sacrifice,' bringing force and conviction to the idea of death as the origin of spiritual power.

Women and Buddhism - Blood Impurity and Motherhood

Nakano Yuko

1. Introduction

The history of Buddhism stretches back 2500 years; yet in spite of its lofty teachings and philosophies, women have clearly been continually suppressed and subjected to sexual discrimination in various forms, practices which are only now being exposed. In my experience of the different sects of Japanese Buddhism, discrimination stems from several roots and has many aspects, which I will illustrate below.

Although sexual discrimination has been present in Buddhist doctrine since the days of the very earliest Indian Buddhism, Japanese Buddhism contains some distinct discriminatory practices and ideas with a long history behind them. According to the rules of conduct for Buddhist priests and priestesses, for example, priestesses were obliged to obey priests in accordance with the eight precepts known as *hakkyoho*. Then there are the *nyonin gosho* (five hindrances of women) which deem that women cannot become Buddha, and *nyonin kekkai*, the sacred areas from which women are excluded and forbidden to set foot in. Many tcmplcs uscd to bar women because of their supposed impurity. It was also difficult for women to perceive the glorification and overemphasis on motherhood within the Buddhist patriarchal concept of family, one that was influenced by nationalistic and commonly accepted perceptions of women. One phenomenon that is only quite recent, *mizuko kuyo*, for instance, is a memorial service for the souls of children who die before birth. It is one example of the sexual discrimination that Buddhism's strong emphasis on motherhood creates, by implanting a strong sense of guilt and wrong-doing in the mother parent only.

As this brief outline illustrates, the nature of sexual discrimination in Japanese Buddhism is complex, and there are various factors which need to be considered in order to understand it. It would be impossible to cover all instances of sexual discrimination in this short space, so I will confine myself to the aforementioned *nyonin kekkai* and assumptions of impurity associated with this, and also touch on the traditional, glorified view of motherhood in Japanese Buddhism.

2. Exclusion of Women and Impurity

Ceremonies and rites barring women's participation have existed in Japan since ancient times, as have religious facilities and sacred areas where they are forbidden to enter. These areas are known as *nyonin kinsei* (women prohibited) or *nyonin kekkai* (women excluded), and are usually enforced at religous sites on mountains or mountain peaks. The number of such sites is decreasing, but the fact they still exist demonstrates how deep-rooted such concepts are. Around Mt. Omine in Nara prefecture, for example, even now there are areas where women are not permitted to climb or worship.

The *nyonin kinsei* designates a sacred zone forbidding women around part, or all, of a mountain or temple. If the zone is violated it is said there will be immediate divine retribution. This belief is illustrated in the *Wakan Sansai Zue*,[1] which contains the tale of a group of aged priestesses who attempted to climb through a taboo area of the holy Tateyama mountain range in Etchu Province (Toyama prefecture), and were turned into stones and cryptomerias. In another tale there was an attempt to build a women's temple in the Tateyama mountains but all the lumber turned into stone. Such legends serve as a warning to all women against violating taboo areas.

Why is it that women were spurned at such length and how can this be accounted for? The answer lies in the concept of impurity, and in

---

[1] Terajima Ryoan edition, Vol.68, Tokyo Bijutsu, Tokyo 1970 reprint. An encyclopedia completed in 1712 and closely patterned on a Chinese work.

particular the concept of women's impurity which Japanese Buddhism persists in clinging to, manifesting itself in the form of the *nyonin kinsei*.

The question then arises as to why women were deemed impure and how did they come to be regarded in this light? One clue can be found in the religious associations known as *ko*. Although there are only a few remaining today, in the past there were many gatherings of these groups, and at their meetings many kinds of poems, called *wasan,* were chanted in praise of Buddhist doctrine and sutras. Amongst them was the following *wasan*, which I have attempted to translate into modern idiom.

The Pool of Blood Hell *Wasan*

Women have the impure water known as menstruation, which defiles the gods when they bathe. The weight of this sin and its retribution are immeasurable, and there is no place where this pollution may be cast away owing to its defilement, therefore it flows into hell and collects in a pool of blood. If a person is born a woman, be she a sovereign wrapped and brought up in brocade, a lady of noble birth or consort of a rich man, even the wife or daughter of a minister or the nobility, or the wife or daughter of a commoner, after death they will all fall into the Pool of Blood Hell and suffer. Then the bodhisattva Avalokitesvara will grant them salvation from this torment.[2]

This *wasan* is an interesting example because of the sense it gives of ancient Japanese perceptions of women; menstruation is deemed impure, and women descend into the Pool of Blood Hell because they defile the gods through menstruation. The inspiration of terror was ingenious by teaching that rank played no part in this fate. Another *wasan* in the same vein was one recited when women die, which also teaches that the gods are defiled through impure menstruation and women must therefore descend into the Pool of Blood Hell. Also included in this *wasan* is the famous thirty fifth vow of the Amida

---

[2] Sotoshu Jinken Yogo Suishin Honbu, Sotoshu Bukkretto - Shukyo to Sabetsu vol.7, Sotoshu Shumucho, 1987.

Buddha describing the Pool of Blood Hell and the Vow for the Salvation of Women.

Women are also restricted by the Five Hindrances (they cannot take precedence over Buddha or other people) and the Three Obediences (to obey their fathers, husbands and sons for support to survive). In short, they should obey men all their lives, and because of these restrictions they also cannot visit sacred places such as Koyasan, the sacred monastic complex of the Shingon sect on Mt. Koya. In both the *wasan* and in these sets of precepts it is deemed a sin to defile the gods with menstrual blood, thus an inherent biological characteristic of women is designated sinful.

The historical document *Ashikura Chugu Onbason Engi* contains a description of the Pool of Blood Hell. This document describes the legend of the principal image in the holy Buddhist mountain temple of Ashikura, an image which takes the form of an old woman called *Onbason*. The sacred peak of Tateyama was also originally prohibited to women, and at the Ashikura temple a Buddhist service, called *Nunohashi daikanjo*, was held for the salvation of women who could neither undertake the mountain pilgrimage nor attain buddhahood. In the legend it is told how the mother of Jiko, the holy priest who opened up Tateyama, fell into the Pool of Blood Hell after death, and there is a description of this Hell.

According to the description, there are three variations of the Pool of Blood Hell. The first, Blood Pool of Doubt, is for those with strong feelings of envy who do not believe in Buddhism; the second, Blood Pool of Wickedness, is for women who are avaricious and do not give alms, are angry towards men, abusive, wilful and immoral. The kind of offenses that lead to the third Self-Heating Blood Pool, are not stated but its terrors are described. And so it is that no woman can escape from either of these three hells. It is significant that women who descend into the second Blood Pool of Wickedness are those who defy men and cause them inconvenience - revealing the true sentiments of a male-centered society here it seems.

The same legend explains why women are condemned to this Hell. Through menstruation and giving birth they expel impure blood which defiles the earth gods; living things on the mountains, in rivers and seas; dwellers of the heavens and dragon gods; Buddhas and the laws of Buddhism itself. In producing such defilement women lead a profoundly sinful existence and therefore must descend into the Pool of Blood Hell. The previous *wasan* shows how strong the notion of menstruation as defilement is, from the fact that menstrual and even birth blood are regarded as polluting. The concept of impurity which originally stemmed from a sense of repugnance towards blood, was expanded to include the source of defilement - women themselves. Thus the descent into hell for individual offenses and retribution came to encompass the entire female sex and the notion of women's impurity spread rapidly.

3. The Ketsubon Sutra

There is one more *wasan* that may have been chanted at *ko* gatherings, and that is the *Ketsubon Kyo Wasan*. In this sutra, the phrase *daiakketsu*, meaning great evil blood, aptly expresses how menstrual and birth blood are regarded. It is taught that women descend into a Pool of Blood Hell formed of the blood which has flowed from themselves, as retribution for the defilement which this *daiakketsu* inflicts on the gods and Buddha. The Ketsubon Sutra is read aloud to attain enlightenement without going to this hell, hence its reputation as the 'women's enlightenment-attaining sutra.' Women were denied salvation because of certain unavoidable biological characteristics regarded as defiling, so the Ketsubon Sutra was devised to get around this dilemma.

Japanese Buddhism continued to spurn women on the one hand while espousing their salvation on the other. It manipulated the logic of the *nyonin kekkai* and created special rites for the sake of women's salvation. The Ketsubon sutra was one part of the overall philosophy on women's salvation, and faith in its efficacy spread across the whole country. But exactly what was the aim of such a philosophy on salvation for women? Judging it to be a manifestation of humanist religious considerations is overly simple. Without going into detail on the proof of this, I believe the conclusion must be drawn that true salvation for women was not actually desired, because it is clear that they only became further marginalised by a notion which appeared to espouse their salvation.

As mentioned earlier, even Buddhist scriptures taught that women could not attain spiritual enlightenment and buddhahood because of the obstacle of the five hindrances. The idea that women could not attain buddhahood has been around since ancient times, and so the theory of *henjonanshi* (metamorphosis of woman into man) was created in order to enable women to attain buddhahood by taking on the form of a man. Thinking about it now, it seems ludicrous that such a theory - women cannot reach buddahood in the form of a woman, but can if they change their body into a man - could go unchallenged. This also did not offer salvation for women in the true sense, because it simply placed them in an inferior position where men could look down from a higher plane of existence and take pity on them.

Jodokyo (Pure Land) Buddhist philosophy contains the idea that a woman's life is one of unrelenting hardship and suffering because of the pain of birth, menstruation, and the burden of life's troubles, and that such a tormented being is excluded from the Pure Land. In other words, women are suffering personified and may not exist there. There is not a single woman to be found in the Pure Land because women, who experience only suffering in the present world, cannot enter there unless they are transformed into men. This may have been a remarkable new means of achieving salvation in the past, but in the present it is nothing more than sexual discrimination borrowing the name of salvation.

The Ketsubon Sutra is currently still regarded as one element of the "salvation policy" devised to save women who are prevented from attaining buddhahood because of defilement. Unlike the the Five Hindrances or *henjonanshi*, however, it is not part of Buddhist doctrine, but was formed from folk religious beliefs by a section of Buddhist priests and ordinary people. It is only a short sutra of around four hundred characters in length, beginning with the hackneyed phrase of Buddhist scriptures, "I have heard that .... ." For the sake of convenience I have attempted to translate this into modern idiom.

The Ketsubon Sutra Preached by Buddha Sakyamuni and Recorded by the Venerable Moggattana

The Venerable Moggattana once saw on a vast plain in Tsuiyo prefecture of U state, a Hell of Blood. Its width was 84,000 *yujun*,[3] and in the centre were 130 kinds of iron chain instruments of torture. Countless numbers of women from the human world, with dishevelled hair and shackles on their wrists, were suffering greatly in that hell. Three times a day the Lord of Hell forces the sinners to drink the unclean blood. If they do not drink he wields an iron bar. Cries of the sinners resound far. Moggattana felt pity and compassion and asked the Lord of Hell: "I can see no men from the human world suffering in this hell. Why is it that so many women only are suffering here?" The Lord of Hell answered Moggattana: "This is something which has no relevance for men. Only women defile the head of the earth gods with blood from giving birth, because they wash blood-soiled clothes in the rivers and pollute the flow. Many good men then draw up that water to boil tea and perform memorial services to various sacred gods, and so the gods have come to hate the defilement of [women's] blood. The great general of heaven announces the names of those who have defiled the earth and rivers, and enters them in the 'Register of Good and Evil.' One hundred years later those women will suffer the torment [of the Blood Hell] for this when they are waiting for their lives to end." Then the Venerable Moggattana used his divine power to proceed immediately to the place where Buddha was. He brought before Buddha the various Buddhist saints, heavenly beings and dragon gods, and the eight guardian deities of Buddha. The Venerable Moggattana told Buddha in great detail of what he had seen, and pleaded: "Lord Buddha, in return for the debt we owe to the mothers who raised us, please explain how they can escape the torments of the Pool of Blood Hell." And Buddha replied: "Your

---

3   One *yujun* equals approximately 7 kilometres. Translator's note

question is indeed natural. I will reveal for you how to repay the debt to your mother. Men and women who love their parents, should respect the three treasures of Buddha, the code, and priests, be self-controlled for three years and sixty days, and worship the name of Buddha. After that, hold a service and invite the priest to read through the [Ketsubon] sutra, and those words of truth will be granted. And if you reflect on your deeds sufficiently, your mother will board the boat of wisdom and be able to cross over the River Sanzu. In the pool of blood a lotus of five colours will appear and all sinners will be greatly overjoyed, a feeling of shame and desire for forgiveness of their sins will arise in their hearts, and instantly they can be reborn in the world of Buddha." Then [Buddha] explained in the [following] words of truth:

"Humbly worship all the Buddhas. Humbly believe in Buddhism. The purity of the precious stone strikes and wins against anything. The Buddha shining over everything and all people have the same pure nature. May there be fortune in the mind of the Enlightened One who shines out over everything. Ah, all people are the same and equal. Ah, and if all people are the same and equal then their true character ought to be pure. Ah, may there be fortune in the blessed light sent forth by Buddha."[4]

Buddha proclaimed to the Venerable Moggattana and various Buddhist saints, "You must disseminate this sutra. If you understand and explain all the teachings of this sutra, [people] will not be deprived [of the teachings of Buddha] even if they have suffered long. Also, if people believe in the Ketsubon Sutra, receive it, read it out and bring others to listen to the explanation, and copy the sutra, then that person's mother in their previous, present and future lives can be reborn in the heavenly world, receive every possible pleasure, and live long and well without wanting for food or clothing. Or, even if the mother dies early, if you believe faithfully in this sutra, she can be saved from the sufferings caused by evil karma and be born into the extremely comfortable Pure Land." The Venerable Moggattana and all

---

[4] See Sakauchi Tatsuo, Shingon Darani, Hirakawa Publishing Co, Tokyo.

the Buddhist saints, the heavenly beings, dragon gods and eight guardian deities listened to Buddha's teaching and received it, then humbly withdrew to worship Buddha.

It is not known exactly when the Ketsubon Sutra was composed, but it is thought to have been composed in China and incorporated into Buddhism as the Gi Sutras via Chinese folk beliefs and the *Dozo*, a canon of Taoism. It appears to have been disseminated widely in China during the Ming and Qing periods, and is thought to have come to Japan around the fifteenth century. In Japan it was originally a scripture for 'women's attaining enlightenment' and was disseminated over a wide area by the Zen Sect known as Soto, attracting women believers across the country. The Shosen Temple of the Soto sect in Motoichibu, Abiko city, Chiba prefecture, became widely known as the 'Appearance of the Ketsubon Sutra Training Hall'. The origin of the sutra is told in the legend of the Shosen Temple Ketsubon Sutra:

During the Oei era (1394-1428) in the town of Abiko in the Minami Soma district of Shimosa Province (now northern Chiba and Ibaraki prefectures), a thirteen year old girl parishioner, the daughter of Hojo Tokiyori, 5th shogun regent of the Kamakura Shogunate, was possessed by the departed spirit of the priestess, Hosho, the founder of the temple. As retribution for the evil karma of a previous life and the defilement of menstruation, Hosho had fallen into the Pool of Blood Hell, where she was in torment. She pleaded for the chief priest of the temple to save her by bestowing the Ketsubon Sutra. When the chief priest prayed to the image of the Jizo bodhisattva, which had been donated by Hojo Tokiyori, the bodhisattva appeared to him in a vision and instructed him to go to the pond. Proceeding there he found that a lotus flower accompanied by the Ketsubon Sutra had appeared. He copied the sutra and read it through, then conducted ceremonial rites for seven days, after which time the spirit of Hosho left the young girl and her sickness was cured. This is the reason why Hosho Temple changed its name to Shosen (Righteous Pond) Temple, and the village name also was changed from Hatto to Ichibu (one part) village because it is said one part of the Ketsubon Sutra gushed out there.[5]

The Ketsubon Sutra was much talked about at the time as news of its virtues and efficacy in saving women from the Pool of Blood Hell spread to surrounding provinces. It was undoubtedly received thankfully by the many women who sought salvation, and accordingly in time was given the status of a Buddhist scripture for the 'salvation' of women in the Soto sect. At some stage it even became incorporated into the sect ceremonies, being conferred on disciples at the *jukai* ceremonies, where they received the commandments of Buddhism. The volume entitled "Showa Teiho Sotoshu Gyoji Kihan" (Showa Revised Standards for Soto Meditation, 1967), directs that the Ketsubon Sutra should be conferred on about the fifth day of the *jukai*, although admittedly this was omitted in the recent 1988 edition because it promoted sexual discrimination. Until 1991 it was conferred at *jukai* ceremonies in the Soji Temple, one of the main peak temples. This same sutra is presently still used by elderly women in some regions as a charm to ward off impurity or as last rite prayers, and is laid in the casket after death.

One commentary on initiation rites, the *Zenmon Jushoku Gyoji Gakuzenshu* (Vol. 8, Komeisha, 1952) states the following in regard to conferral of the Ketsubon Sutra on around the fifth day of ceremonies:

> Circulation of the meditation hall after breakfast is as for the previous day. The morning repast finishes and after circulating the hall the Ketsubon Sutra is conferred. Because women feel the deep sin of ascending the dais to receive the precepts in an impure state, they will feel at ease after this is conferred.

The assumption here that not only are women impure, but that they themselves also feel this impurity to be a profound sin, illustrates how men's sense of repugnance towards the blood expelled during menstruation, birth and its so-called impurity, has been greatly magnified so that women have come to regard themselves as impure.

---

[5] From Sotoshu Zensho, Zenkai, Komeisha, 1972, Ketsubon Sutra Yushutsu Enyu Suishu, Kaike Rakusodan.

This commentary also describes methods of conferring the Ketsubon Sutra and making a Ketsubon Sutra protection charm. Although the sutra was conferred on all women who participated in the initiation ceremonies on the occasions it was conferred, it was not necessarily conferred on every occasion, although it did seem to have happened quite frequently.

A sermon given at a *jukai* ceremony held by the Soto sect at the end of the Edo era also mentions the Ketsubon Sutra. Examples of its efficacy were given, such as; how spirits of the dead have pleaded for the sutra; dreams of how women were saved from falling into the Pool of Blood Hell after death by praying for protection by the Ketsubon Sutra; or how the pain of menstruation was avoided by protecting themselves with the Ketsubon Sutra and how by wearing the charm on the body, defilement is avoided and they can worship at a shrine or temple. In essence, the function of the Ketsubon Sutra as a protection against impurity and the notion that women are impure, was made crystal clear.

In the same sermon the following was also related: The chief priest of a certain temple had ordered a new temple bell to be cast and a woman was pumping the bellows to smelt the metal, but somehow it would not dissolve. At the suggestion of another priest they threw a Ketsubon Sutra into the bellows and it apparently went well after that. The implication is, of course, that the sutra cancelled the woman's impurity; the notion of women's impurity and efficacy of the Ketsubon Sutra are expounded, demonstrating how the situation arose whereby priests and people came to accept such a concept without resistance. Through repeatedly hearing sermons stressing the idea, women themselves came to believe that they were impure and thus profoundly sinful, and believed they could not be saved unless they had recourse to the Ketsubon Sutra.

One of the important religious points passed from master to disciple in the Soto sect on slips of paper called *shitsunaikirigami*, was that women's menstrual blood is impure. Therefore, when participating in festivals and *jukai* ceremonies they had to wear a special charm on the body or swallow it, so as not to spread the blood defilement around them. It is interesting that there are two kinds of these paper charms, one to temporarily stop menstruation and the other a charm to return the temporarily stopped menstruation to normal, in effect functioning in the same role as modern drugs which regulate the menstrual cycle. I wonder how many women of that time were forcibly inconvenienced in their actual daily lives simply because of this notion of the impurity of menstrual blood?

4. Development of the Concept of Blood Defilement

When considering the notion of blood defilement and women's impurity, the question arises as to how this concept came about. Historically, it is not clear exactly when and how the concept came into being, but Nishiguchi Junko has postulated that its origins in Japan arose from Shinto and later spread to Buddhism.[6] Another theory is that Buddhism introduced blood defilement into Japanese culture, but the influence of fortune-telling and divination in creating strong feelings of taboo in nobles of the Heian era, could also conceivably have reinforced ideas regarding blood defilement. Yet the question still remains as to why Japanese people came to regard blood, particularly menstrual and birth blood, as defiling in the first place.

There has been much discussion of the subject in fields such as cultural anthropology. Cultural anthropologist Namihira Emiko wrote in reference to the idea of menstrual and birth blood as impure, that it arose through a "great inversion of values," and "contact with something belonging to a different category," and because this was a "vague classification somewhere in the middle," it was taken to be "a physiologically abnormal state" and thus caused "a physiological impact on the persons concerned and other people in the vicinity."[7] It seems then, that perceptions of menstrual and childbirth blood as

---

[6] Nishiguchi Junko, Onna no Chikara - Kodai no Josei to Bukkyo, Heibonsha Ltd., Tokyo 1987.

[7] Namihira Emiko, Kegare no Kozo, Seidosha, Tokyo, 1988.

impure, arose from the idea that women are intrinsically different to men, and thus forced them into a position where they are regarded as impure. A male dominated society in which women are seen as instrinsically different would interpret biological characteristics not possessed by the dominant group as abnormal, thus feeding a primitive fear which led them to regard menstruation and birth as impure. Such a society would have felt there was a certain kind of 'power' in menstrual blood which threatened their vested rights, and out of fear labelled it as pollution to suppress and seal off its 'power'. Namihira quotes M. Douglas' explanation in regard to this 'power,' that pollution is one kind of power which has the strength to render impure anything it comes in contact with, and through the impurity of women, gives them one kind of power over men.[8] In the previously mentioned *Onbason Engi*, however, blood was thought harmful for people and both heavenly beings and dragon gods will suffer from the five marks of decay and three sufferings of a dragon; therefore it is also likely that menstrual and birth blood were believed to have the power to harm the gods. The end result is that women themselves, the source of this 'harm', came to be perceived as impure.

5. Ideological Maternalism - The Glorified Mother

Apart from blood defilement, there is one more issue that must be touched on that has until now been completely neglected by male-centred Buddhist sects, namely issues related to motherhood.

If the word motherhood is mentioned, then stories of high priests and their mothers spring to mind. The most famous of these is about the Venerable Moggattana of the Ketsubon Sutra, who saved his mother from the torments of becoming a hungry ghost. This tale is also the origin of the Bon Festival (Urabon'e) in Japan, held every summer to welcome the spirits of ancestors back to earth for a short time, and is described in the *Urabon'e* Sutra. In many commentaries,

---

8 Namihira Emiko, ibid., underlining in original.

however, the reason given for Moggattana's mother descending into hell is because her love for her son was so great that she treated other people coldly. This tale is used to illustrate the egotistic side of motherhood, and is often quoted in sermons as an example of the power of maternal love. But is this really the role of maternalism? What are maternal qualities and what does motherhood really mean? Consider the following:

> ... even if equal numbers of men and women are assumed, I think it is right to say that all men, without exception, are part of woman. The reason being that all people are born of a mother. And they are brought up by their mother. From this alone, it can be said that people are part of their mothers and belong to their mothers ...[9]

This is an extract from the Soto sect's guide for proselytising, in which all women are designated as 'mothers,' hence sanctifying their role and accentuating the nuance that women are a 'species of mothers'. It follows that responsibility for raising children is therefore shifted to women as the 'mothers', and seems to indicate that all women are unconditionally thought to have the maternal affection that qualifies them as mothers. We could infer then that a major reason why existing Buddhist sects cannot eliminate intrinsic sexual discrimination is because such a concept of motherhood is an obstacle.

In Japan there is a certain emotion and mystique surrounding motherhood. Many Japanese men have what could almost be called a kind of religious feeling about motherhood, or are caught up by the image. It is an image of 'magnanimous mother love,' 'all-embracing mother love' and the 'mother who gives birth to everything.' The maternal nature of women therefore has come to be seen as innate, a quality which women themselves too have come to believe in.

Definitions of maternalism are varied, and there is still no established one. Of the considerable research that has been done on the subject, too numerous to list here, the medical definition is a significant one that is worth noting. This is limited to women in a state

---

[9] Nakano Toei, Fujin no tame no Fukyo, Sotoshu Fukyo Shido Sosho, Vol. 2, Sanbo Shoin, 1953.

of pregnancy, childbirth, confinement or breastfeeding, and the physical features that distinguish their ability to give birth and breastfeed. Maternalism was originally limited to the biological characteristics of pregnancy, childbirth and breastfeeding only, yet it has rapidly come to be widely interpreted as synonymous with the female gender. In recent years there has been a tendency to broaden the definition beyond a medical basis to include a value laden interpretation of love for children which is now treated as an instinctual natural gift. Thus the demarcation between the medical concept of maternalism and that of common understanding has disappeared.[10] In this concept of maternalism the mother parent is not regarded as an individual, giving greater force to the view of the mother-child relationship as a sacred area, and further tightening the social bonds between mother and child.

Ebara Yumiko has categorised maternalism by dividing it into "the physical functions of motherhood," "actions of motherhood" and "idea of motherhood." According to Ebara there are positive aspects of maternalism and negative aspects, with the third group, the "idea of motherhood", falling into the latter category. She has called this "ideological motherhood" and links it to sexual discrimination. Being abstract, conceptual and ideological, it encompasses the previously mentioned so-called universal features of maternalism. The expression that 'motherhood can save the world and stop war' surely stems from this notion, and signifies the concept of a life of selfless love which asks nothing in return.[11]

The ideology of maternalism has become a convenient concept for modern Japanese society. The unpaid work of child rearing is shouldered by women as a matter of course, freeing male workers to devote themselves to paid work in the public sphere. In modern male-centered society women are approved of only when they display 'maternalism'. Generally speaking, the maternal ideology of modern

---

[10] Ohinata Masami, Bosei no Kenkyu - Sono Keisei to Henyo no Katei, Dentoteki Boseikan he no Hansho, Kawashima Shoten, 1988.

[11] Ebara Yumiko, Ribu no Shucho to Boseikan, in Bosei wo Kaidoku Suru - Tsukurareta Shinwa wo Koete, Yuhikaku, Tokyo, 1991.

and contemporary society can be conceptualised as "woman = mother = nature."[12]

Men and male-dominated society have unconsciously replaced women's biological differences with cultural differences, so that by assigning women to the position of 'nature,' as opposed to its polar opposite, 'culture,' or to the middle ground in between the two, they have created a schematics of 'culture = male, nature = female.' Typical of the thinking which views women as a birth-giving sex of mothers, is that which conceptualises nature as 'mother earth' and 'female'. Beliefs in fertility and earth mother deities are common throughout the world and have helped to form an image of women as mothers.

Although menstruation and birth continue to be seen as impure and feared, women cannot be totally excluded or continuation of the species would not be possible. They are the birth-giving gender and in this sense their gender is 'positive' and possibly a threat to male domination and initiative. To maintain their grip on leadership, men have had to categorise women as having inferior values, and for this to succeed it was necessary for them to denigrate the reproductive capacity of women, even if it is vital for continuation of the human race. This has been an unconscious rather than a conscious process, and precisely because of that, women themselves have not been aware of the assumptions and stereotypes which were shaping their lives.

Funabashi Keiko refers to the relationship between maternal ideology and the view that "woman = nature" in pointing out that motherhood ideology functions as a device of women's oppression, and stresses that in order to come to grips with maternal ideology it is important to clearly delineate maternalism and maternal ideology. She raises the alarm on Japanese-style mother-child relations, particularly in the case of boy children, in which mother and child are glued tightly together by social constraints, and lists the characteristics of maternal ideology in Japan as; (1) a strong awareness of role and labour

---

[12] Funabashi Keiko, 'Bosei' Gainen no Saikento 'Bosei no Shakaigaku,' Saiensusha, Tokyo, 1992.

division according to gender, (2) a child-centered principle, and (3) a lack of distance in human relations.[13]

Consider also the following: "... it seems that it is the boundless love of the Kanzeon bodhisattva, eternally benevolent and constant, which guides us through the polished wisdom handed down, that is our eternal maternalism."[14] In this quotation maternalism is regarded as synonymous with the love of a boddhisattva. The words 'impartial, devotion, unselfish, harmony, stability and natural' are often used in conjunction with the description of this bodhisattva, and are revealing of the Japanese image of maternalism. Often in publications distributed and used by various religious groups, the self-sacrificing maternal love of women is praised and there is a great amount of material urging women to be self-sacrificing mothers.

The short-sightedness of categorising Buddhism as 'the mother's religion,' must furthermore add to the risk of a concealed *hongaku* philospohy. *Hongaku* is the concept of enlightenment being a priori, that is immanent in all things-as-they-are as opposed to gradual enlightenment which must be worked for. The first use of it was discovered in the *Daijo Kishinron* (Treatise on the Awakening of Faith in the Mahayana), which greatly influenced Mahayana Buddhism, and developed mainly in the Japanese Tendai Sect around the key words and concepts of *hongaku*, meaning original enlightenment. As a Buddhist philosophy *hongaku* has great value as an extremely advanced theory, yet it affirms the idea that even ordinary people leading muddled lives are Buddha, and are a form of the true Buddha living in the present, a theory said to be a departure from Buddhism. The Japanese tendency to accept reality positively has close connections to such philosophy. *Hongaku* thought is linked to the traditional latter half of the Lotus Sutra used in the Tendai Sect temple on Mt. Hiei, where Japanese thought on reality affirmation was incorporated and a thorough philosophical system of reality was created. This was later re-incorporated into Japanese thought and used

---

[13] Funabashi Keiko, ibid.

[14] Ebe Oson, Kuon no Haha in Byakugo, Meicho Fukyu Kai, Tokyo, reissued 1985.

as a theoretical framework in areas of culture such as *sado* (tea ceremony), *kado* (flower arrangement) and *nogaku* (noh theatre). Women's studies researchers and a section of Buddhist researchers have, in recent years, frequently pointed out that *hongaku* philosophy as represented by 'Japanism' is one cause of the discriminatory perceptions of maternalism and women in Japan.[15]

The key idea of *hongaku* philosophy is that ordinary people possess a priori enlightenment and are Buddha, therefore religious training is also not necessary, clearly expressed in the phrase "*bonno soku bodai,*" meaning that ordinary people stained with worldly desires are a form of Buddha as they are, so there is in essence no gap between the two. *Hongaku* is a philosophy that clearly accepts and affirms reality, and as such it is linked to a fatalistic and popular idea of karma that makes the salvation of women even more difficult to achieve. It does offer a slight chance for women to attain buddhahood but in actual fact because of the karma of the previous life and sins of women's defilement in this life, that chance is cancelled out and women are supposed to sink into the Pool of Blood Hell after death.

Because there are such strong fixed perceptions of ideological maternalism in Japan, men naturally, and women too, are unconsciously and unquestioningly brought under the compelling 'spell' of motherhood. As with almost all other gender discriminations, motherhood continues to be unconsciously and mistakenly accepted by the general public as a custom or national characteristic. This ideological notion of motherhood was brought about by the currents in thinking of a male-dominated society, and any critics of it were rejected. Moreover, the idea became firmly secured and was transformed into generally accepted thinking. Subsequently it has been difficult to gain an objective hearing of critical opinions from women's point of view, because this has nearly always been linked to a denial of their own female sexuality. The topic verged on taboo. Yet, as Ikeda Shoko has stated, "the entire gamut of human relations which should

---

[15] Tamura Yoshiro, Tamura Yoshiro Bukkyo Ronshu, vol.1 Hongakushisoron, Shunjusha, Tokyo, 1990. Iwanami Bukkyojiten, Iwanami Shoten, Tokyo, 1989.

be mutually fostered, will denigrate into a relationship of mere compromise and spoiling,"[16] therefore for the sake of both sexes it is important to continue the critique of wrongful notions of motherhood engendered by ideological maternalism.

Discrimination and distorted perceptions of motherhood in Buddhism do not all have their roots in Buddhist doctrine, and it is apparent that other factors, including common understanding and generally accepted ideas in society; the state structure; and the values of the religious leaders who pass this on, have also all contributed. That which is called the Buddhist view of motherhood, has always been swayed by the trends of the times and the views of individual religious leaders. A philosophy glorifying and overemphasising motherhood was planted in the scriptures in the form of general understanding, and amplified in the perceptions of women and motherhood by those who transmit this philosophy. Under the further influence of social customs and varying trends in thought, it eventually became confused with doctrine, a doctrine which is further disseminated through proselytising or communicated to the general populace in a religious form. In this way social and ideological perceptions of motherhood were transmitted to society and sexual discrimination was perpetuated.

6. Eliminating Sexual Discrimination - The Problem of Japanese Buddhism

It is important to realise that notions of blood defilement and views of maternalism are amplified and transmitted by those who proselytise. Sexual discrimination engendered by perceptions of women's impurity together with an ideologically prejudiced view of motherhood, has also been amplified and sustained by religious leaders. Notions of women's impurity and the glorification of motherhood were

---

[16] Ikeda Shoko, 'Onna' 'Haha' Sore zore no Shinwa - Komi, Kosodate, Kazoku no ba kara, Akashi Shoten, Tokyo, 1990.

increasingly stressed in the sermons and discourses of priests, inducing women themselves to believe in the burden of their so-called sinful existence and destiny as mothers.

Until now, views of women's salvation in Japanese Buddhism have always been closely connected to views of women's sins and an ideologically prejudiced view of motherhood. The Ketsubon Sutra became a scripture for 'women's attaining buddhahood' and 'women's salvation' because women believed that it could exempt them from the sin of blood defilement. But Buddhist sects took advantage of this to glorify only motherhood, while at the same time shunning the most integral aspects of birth and menstruation as polluting - an ingenious method that extolled women on the one hand while denigrating them on the other. Faith in the Ketsubon Sutra was, it turns out, a theory of women's salvation postulated from a position of male superiority. Belief in its efficacy spread because it played upon the anxieties of women whose fate was to descend into Hell due to the defilement of their blood, and Buddhist proselytisers still continue to skilfully play on these anxieties. This is unforgivable, even if it is under a banner of compassion; compassion ought not to be pointless and true mercy would be to recognise women as equals. Furthermore, if the impulse to denigrate women did stem from a fear of the 'power' of menstrual or birth blood, from a contemporary viewpoint this cannot be an excuse for the shunning of women, and from feminist and contemporary human rights perspectives it can certainly no longer go unchallenged. When I stated earlier that such a means of salvation could not be a true salvation, it was on these grounds.

Buddhism has been in Japan for approximately 1,500 years. Originally a foreign religion, it has become firmly rooted, adapted, and has now settled into the form of a conventional native religion. Discriminatory ideas were brought to Japan with Buddhism, but through Japanisation of the religion, these ideas were combined with ancient discriminatory concepts to form a unique Japanese style of Buddhism in which discriminatory customs evolved over time. To be sure there have been consideration and efforts to eliminate discrimination, but these attempts have been limited. The teachings of

Buddhism, supposed to be about true salvation, were linked to the political powers of the ages and became part of the mechanisms of discrimination, continuing to spawn victims and repeat oppression. On the whole, Japanese Buddhism has evolved with a tendency to embrace contradictions that have fostered discrimination, so that contemporary Buddhism in Japan is now forced into the situation where it must confront this.

The time has already passed when existing Buddhist groups can rest idly on unchanging and outdated structures, and the age is approaching when both men and women and groups should be reconsidering their faith and the road to salvation. Exposure to much severe criticism has enabled the history of Japanese Buddhism to be reviewed with new eyes. Buddhists and Buddhist groups should seriously listen to such opinions and search for the road to a true Buddhist rebirth.

Meeting Christian Women in Sixteenth Century Japan

Iwata Sumie

1. Introduction

Christianity first reached Japan with Francisco Xavier when he arrived in Kagoshima on August 15th, 1549. Over the next hundred years or so until its prohibition, Christianity flourished alongside the Portugese and Spanish culture that accompanied it. A hundred years is three or four generations, long enough for people to be born and raised in a completely Christian environment, which is what some regions became.

Historically speaking, the people who are known as *kirishitan* (Christians) were Catholics, and as a Protestant I did not feel a deep affinity with them. I knew from history that long ago people who converted to Catholicism were cruelly persecuted, but I had never heard anything about them at Protestant Churches and other Christian gatherings, and even after seeing dramatisations of novels written by Catholic authors, I still felt that they were alien and unrelated to me. Then, as I came to think more about the Japanese people and religion, I became curious about, and felt a need to know how Japanese women had first reacted to Christianity, differing so much as it does from Shinto or Japanese Buddhism. While reading about the cruel persecution and martyrdom of early Japanese Christians, I discovered that in 1623 at the crossroads known as *Fuda no Tsuji* in Edo (as Tokyo was then known) as many as 50 priests and believers were burned at the stake. *Fuda no Tsuji* is close to present day Japan Railway's Tamachi Station and the Mita subway station, and is now a thoroughfare crossed by heavy traffic. It is very close to a Quaker girls school where I used to work, and I had passed through the area everyday unaware of its historical significance.

The gulf between Protestants and Catholics had made me ignorant of and indifferent to this part of history I believe. Realisation of the awfulness of this was a long time in coming. Fifty people gave their lives for the Christian faith, but in later generations I passed over the site of their martyrdom without giving them a thought, without grieving for their fate. It makes light of their deaths, and even renders them pointless.

My complicity in letting such an historical event sink so shamefully into oblivion was, I felt, unforgivable, and I wanted to make their lives and deaths meaningful again by coming to terms with their cries from the past.

As a woman with an interest in feminist theology, my need to know more about the Christian women of the past was compelling, but with the exception of a tiny handful of famous figures such as Hosokawa Gracia (1563-1600) and Mother Julia (who was a Korean), there has been almost no discussion of ordinary Christian women in Japan. In literature, the novels that have been written are overwhelmingly concerned with priests, male believers, or the mission of young boys sent to Europe in the sixteenth century. The thorough persecution and rooting out of Christians in earlier centuries, however, meant that there was little or no documentation of their lives left in Japan. Why were they excluded with such enmity? Toyotomi Hideyoshi's intentions in prohibiting Christianity are still not clear. Fear of colonisation by western powers is one theory, but this does not explain why the Tokugawa shogunate left no stone unturned in searching out and killing all Christians, after barring western priests and other foreigners from the country. It must have been because of exposure to the 'dangerous ideas' of Christianity itself, fears which the Amakusa and Shimabara revolts of 1637 proved to be justified in some respects.

At any rate, the paucity of Japanese sources meant there was no choice but to use western ones for my research, and so the information for this paper is drawn from a book entitled *Nihonshi* (Historia de Iapam). This is a work written by Luis Frois, a Jesuit priest who was in Nagasaki from 1563 until his death in 1597 (except for the period

1592-95 when he was in Macau), and is limited to the women mentioned in volumes VI to VIII, known as the *Bungohen*.[1]

According to the translator, Matsuda Kiichi, the first part of *Nihonshi* up to chapter 41 is contained in the three volumes of *Bungohen*, and corresponds with the beginning of a treatise on the history of the Japanese Church. It is evident from the chronology that this section was not entirely written from Frois' direct experience, however, his "whole object in writing *Nihonshi* in the first place was not to leave new historical records for later generations of Japanese historians, but to show how much hardship the first missionaries in sixteenth century Japan experienced, and how Christians were exemplary in their devotion to their faith, so in this sense it can be said that the *Bungohen* is a good example of the nature of *Nihonshi*."[2]

In 1556 missions spread relatively early to Bungo because the church in nearby Yamaguchi prefecture was burnt down in war. The Daimyo (feudal lord) of Bungo, Otomo Sorin, was drawn to Christianity early on and was christened in 1576 taking the name Francisco. Soon after his baptism in 1578, the Bungo army was completely destroyed by Shimazu Yoshihisa at Takajo in Hyuga (present day Miyazaki prefecture).

2. Women Possessed

Frois wrote that "In Bungo at that time, possessions of people were indeed frequent, and through the driving out of evil spirits by our Lord God, the great miracle he has bestowed upon us is made known publicly."[3] He notes many records of people possessed by evil spirits and driven mad, or wracked by sickness. But these people were returned to normal, cured of sickness and found faith through

---

[1] The volumes named after Bungo, former name for the greater part of present-day Oita prefecture. Translated by Matsuda Kiichi and Kawasaki Touta, Chuo Koronsha, Tokyo 1978.

[2] From the introduction to volume 6.

[3] Nihonshi, vol. 7, p.94.

administering the exorcism ceremony, sprinkling holy water and saying prayers, just like in the Gospels or The Acts of the Apostles. There were many recorded instances of possession of women in particular, varying in rank from complete unknowns to the wives of nobles.

In one case many people had gathered to hear the word of God, whereupon a mad woman entered and "caused a wild disturbance with mad ravings and rampaging, and it seemed no one could hear the sermon because of it." In another instance a thirty year old high-ranking woman "suffering from evil spirits" (the sister of Shiga Don Paulo mentioned below), came to the priest saying that she wanted to become a Christian. After having been taught to chant the words of prayer she began to intone, "'If they [the Padres] damn my Buddhism, Sakyamuni [Gautama Buddha] and Amitabha, there would be nothing to pray to. There is no one who can conquer this [evil]. I will not pray to anyone.'" Then, "on the next day, which was the festival day of the Virgin Mary, the priest offered mass to the many Christians who had gathered, and after it was over he asked the woman several questions. Everyone then began to pray, and after a while the evil spirit left her completely, and the woman asked for a drink. People gave her holy water and asked her to intone 'Jesus, Mary, San Miguel', and she began to chant softly. At this the people recognised that the evil spirit had left her and everyone gave thanks to God. And the evil spirit never came back to her."[4]

"The wife of a nobleman, a retainer of the ruler of Bungo .... was tormented by evil spirits and was always leaving the house to go to nearby fields where she screamed out fearful things." This woman was admitted to the first hospital in Japan, built in 1557 by the missionaries, and "no sooner had her fits subsided and the time that the evil spirits held her in their torment been cut, than her spirit became completely free and lucid." On the day of baptism, the evil spirits tormented her once more with a terrible attack, but "the Lord granted that she would never again be seized with the physical agony

---

[4] Vol. 6, pp. 134-5.

and suffering that had tormented her." At this point "her husband begged the [Bungo] Daimyo for permission to become a Christian." The Daimyo had no objections in giving permission, saying that he desired all his retainers to become Christians. The husband then went immediately with his son, daughter and retainers to hear a sermon and all received the Holy Baptism together.[5]

An old woman possessed by evil spirits for 18 years, was present while a priest was explaining "the significance of the Redemption, and he came to the part about the son of God being nailed to the Cross, whereupon the old woman suddenly started trembling and with both hands clutching her sides pouted her lips, and little by little lost her human countenance, her face becoming sharp and ugly and taking on the features of a dog."[6]

The wife of Yoshinori, an enemy of Christians despite being the son of Daimyo Francisco, "had been badly troubled by a kind of sleeping sickness for four or five years. This evil spirit tormented her inordinately and the wretched woman had become mere skin and bones, paralyzed as it were, unable to move and tormented by hallucinations. Because of this [she] used up all her possessions to pay for Buddhist monks and exorcisms. But far from her suffering being cured by the Buddhist monks, it increased daily. She had previously heard Christian stories, and under the persuasion of her sisters-in-law Marcencia and Regina, the daughters of Don Francisco, earnestly desired to become a Christian and to be freed from the sleeping sickness, but was not able to do so because she was prevailed on by her husband."[7] The old woman and the wife were both subsequently saved.

When a married man brought his crazy wife to the church in Bungo, the priest was talking, but the Christians gathered there chanted The Lords Prayer in loud voices and "the woman began to tremble so violently that even three men could not stop it. Thereupon some

---

[5] Ibid., pp. 258-9.

[6] Vol. 8, p. 34.

[7] Ibid., p. 271.

people sprinkled holy water on her while another person continued intoning prayers. And in doing this, by the will of Our Lord God, she was released [from the evil spirit] and piously began calling out the holy names of Jesus and Mary, saying her breast had been greatly oppressed for seven years. After receiving solace, [the couple] resolved to return to the church [on another day] to hear the preaching and receive baptism, and left toward morning."[8]

3. Women Believers

Many women from a wide social strata became believers and decided to receive baptism. There are numerous accounts of people who converted because they felt they could truly understand the teachings and were content to believe. Some women of the time devoted themselves to directly coming to grips with the teachings of this new religion, women such as the Christian maidservant of a certain high ranking man of Hirado (Dejima), who was a Buddhist. The master announced that she must renounce this faith immediately or be killed. She answered, "I became a Christian, and it is not to abandon faith and become a heathen again" and because she "went out to worship the cross," her master killed her.[9]

The mother of a young girl who had already converted to Christianity, "had never become a Christian because she was afraid of relatives and public opinion," but "through prayer and counsel" her daughter was able to take her to a priest and lead her into becoming a believer.[10]

The wife of one esteemed Christian "was a great heathen and the sister of a Buddhist monk, and had no intention of becoming a Christian because she believed in the religion of her brother. But as the result of "hearing about God for several days" for certain reasons, she

---

[8] Vol. 6, p. 144.
[9] Vol. 6, p. 224.
[10] Vol. 7, pp. 50-1.

visited a priest and "earnestly implored" him, "Father, do not leave us as heathens. Do not prolong any longer granting us baptism. We already understand the truth [of Christianity], and recognise there is no other salvation. ... And as she spoke tearfully out of a deep faith, the priest had to grant her reasonable petition."[11]

An old woman who died in 1565 in a certain city of Bungo "was a Christian for 15 years. She had a great many children who were all heathens, and one brother who was a Buddhist priest and extremely powerful in that land. Not one of them dared to meet the old woman, simply because she was a Christian." She did not care about this and continued in her life of faith. But "when the old woman was dying, the children and Buddhist priest brother tried very hard to lead her astray, sending a messenger asking for permission to visit." She answered, "I have been a Christian for 15 years and have endured much poverty in recent years. But because I am Christian people have not come to visit me or help me. So I have endured this with the love of Jesus Christ, and even when there was deep winter snow I woke early and went to Church, always entrusting this body to the Lord who created me. At this time I would plead with my God to weigh this service and not to deprive me of my rewards as a pious Christian. I am fully aware that your honourable selves are conspiring and respectfully request you not to visit."[12]

There was also the following spirited narrative: "A certain noble and respected woman was greatly angered at a female servant one day during Lent that year. [However] by the afternoon she regretted her anger and as atonement followed the example of Christ and washed the feet of all her female servants. This was an extrremely strange and uncommon thing among Japanese."[13]

---

[11] Ibid., p. 51.

[12] Ibid., p. 52.

[13] Vol. 8, p. 316.

4. *Isabel and Magdalena*

There are two women mentioned in the *Bungohen* who leave a particularly strong impression. One is Nata, the first wife of Daimyo Otomo Sorin, who maintained a strong opposition to Christianity and was given the nickname of Isabel by the Jesuits, after the Israeli queen, wife of Ahab, who oppressed the prophets and forced the people to worship Baal. Nata actively tried to distance the Otomo heir, Yoshimune, from the teachings of Christianity and "return to the traditional religion of our ancestors."

A contrasting picture to Isabel is that of Magdalena, the wife of Shiga no Taro (Don Paulo). Frois wrote that "she was a distinguished woman in the land of Bungo; through baptism in the name of our Holy Lord, she was bestowed an especial bond with the Lord. Apart from that, she was from the first a splendid person of various talents and great sensibility, which were all the more fitting preparation for the spirit to receive the grace of God. To this day, all the priests and brothers who attended to that castle returned with admiration for her oustanding virtue, manner and chasteness, presiding splendidly over the affairs of the house in spite of being still only a young woman."[14]

Her mother-in-law, the daughter of the notorious Isabel, pressured her son and Magdalena to renounce their religion, and blamed Magdalena for the death of their first child from sickness, saying "this must be yours and Don Paulo's punishment from Buddha and the gods for abandoning them and becoming Christians." "Magadalena promptly replied, 'From this time onwards I must be an even better Christian. ... the only path to be with my child in the next world is to fulfill my life as a good Christian.'"[15] Her husband, Don Paulo, was firm of faith and so it was easy for the mother-in-law to see her daughter-in-law as a comparatively easy target to attack and criticise, but Magdalena's answer was brave and unwavering; "Now for example, even if Don Paulo and the retainers were to abandon the

---

[14] Vol. 8, p. 124.
[15] Ibid., pp. 126-7.

[Christian] teachings, I absolutely could not follow their example. Please acknowledge that I will not abandon the truth and teachings which have spiritually awakened me."[16]

The priests thought Don Paulo was helped because "Our Lord God has bestowed on him a like companion, but as people say, a woman who also surpasses him in her knowledge of God." Frois wrote further that "despite being struck with the aforemetioned tragic anguish, in the space of a few months after baptism, through the will of God it came to pass that she accepted it with great restraint and an unchanging heart."[17]

The Satsuma army reached Bungo in their advance, and Don Paulo and Magdalena escaped alone by fleeing through the unknown terrain in the mountains for two nights and days to reach Kiyota castle. "The Christians there received no small impression of Don Paulo's and Magdalena's faith and virtue" wrote Frois, but added mischievously however, that their flight was difficult because of Magdalena's large girth.[18]

5. Spiritual Journies of Christian Women

Frois' *Bungohen* describes various Christian women, but it goes beyond a simple tale of faith in its portrayal of women confronting the new teachings independently and in earnest. In this period of history women were not recognised as human beings, and the many recorded instances of their possession by evil spirits during the extremely uncertain times of the Sengoku period,[19] were caused no doubt by the destruction of a spiritual equilibrium. It seems possible that Buddhism of the time was not a real means of salvation for people. Some women exhausted all their money to pay for Buddhist monks and exorcists, only to find their troubles and sicknesses uncured and deepening

---

[16] Ibid., pp. 126-6.

[17] Ibid., p. 131.

[18] Ibid., p. 178.

[19] 1467-1568, also known as the Warring States period. Translator's note.

confusion. The woman who clamored and rampaged in a place where many people came to worship; the woman who went into a field everyday to scream out in a fearful voice; what is it they wanted in their heart of hearts? There must have been some impulse which drove them to scream. Some became Christians with their husbands, but what of the rest of their lives? The new Christian teachings seem to have healed not only spiritually, but physically as well. For many women, it was therefore not a partial salvation, but one that gave holistic health.

Catholic orthodoxy would have it that people not healed by Buddhist monks and faith healers, were returned to normality through Christianity, but I think there is more to it than this. The records state that it is as if they were saved directly by "calling out the name of Jesus and Mary."[20] In the very early stages, when the missionaries were still hampered by their lack of fluency in Japanese and it is not clear whether the doctrine was adequately communicated or not, it seems a strong belief in God, the Lord creator of all things on heaven and earth, the Saviour Lord Jesus, and Mary who interecedes, strongly penetrated hearts of the believers. It was not like the Shinto belief in eight million deities, or Buddhist beliefs in Buddha, Bodhisattvas and Nyorai, but faith in a man called Jesus and his mother, a woman called Mary, and thus, one imagines, something infinitely more intimate. Strictly speaking, Mary is a human being not a god, but since the very early stages of Christianity, people have seemed dissatisfied with only a male god, and the longing for a female god was fulfilled by Mary. People always demand the male and female elements in their lives, and this was reflected in their image of god. The Hidden Christians[21] worship of Maria Kannon, Mother of Mercy, can be recalled as an example of *kirishitan's* particular leaning, and must be remembered in this context. The notion of a sole transcendent god, called Deus,

---

[20] San Miguel, whose name was also called out, was the guardian saint of Japan.

[21] Christians who concealed their belief and went underground after the anti-Christian edicts of the Tokugawa shogunate. Translator's note.

creator of the whole world including one individual, would have left a deep impression on sixteenth century Japanese.

The single-minded attitude apparent from the beginning of this era until the later period of persecution, was striking, and people were willing to risk their lives to protect the faith. A servant unhesitatingly answered her master that "I became a Christian and there is no reason for me to abandon my faith and become a heathen again" - and was killed for it. An old woman refused to see her children and brother because she had become a Christian, and could endure until death "because of the love of Jesus Christ."

There is something in the description of the noblewoman washing the feet of her attendants which leaps across four hundred years to strike a chord in me. The origin of her act can be found in the Gospel according to St. John, when Jesus stood up from the table where he was taking supper with the apostles before facing death, washed their feet and dried them with his own hands. This woman severely scolded her female servant for some reason, but later when she had calmed down, realised it was trivial, and it was the very important season of Lent. She deeply regretted her actions and therefore followed Jesus' example with the apostles by washing the feet of not just that one servant, but all her female servants. She literally followed the words of Christ, who said "As your master and teacher I have washed your feet and so you must also wash each others feet." Frois nonchalantly adds that "this was singularly uncommon and unheard of amongst Japanese people." In this action was realised symbolically and actually, the essential equality of people regardless of position, which is at the core of Christian thought.

The dignified independence of Magdalena, whom Frois admired so much, shone through in the words, "I would absolutely not comply with that, please accept that I cannot abandon the teachings and truth which have spiritually awakened me," even if her husband and all retainers decided to abandon Christianity. Bearing in mind that this is a reply to the threats of her mother-in-law, it is clear that Christianity had already become irreplaceable for Magdalena. For her there was probably nothing more to fear. There are many more examples of such dauntless women in Christianity's troubled history in Japan.

The idea of male and female chastity left a strong impression on Hideyoshi and Nobunaga. The idea of one wife to one husband as an immutable ethic was presented to Japanese men who at the time did not even think of women as human beings. Later persecution of Christians is said to be related to Toyotomi Hideyoshi's anger at Christian women who would not yield themselves to him.

There is no doubt that the Christian view of male/female relations must have given enormous joy to oppressed women. They received it as a gift of life and it is easy to understand how they would have regarded it as more precious than anything else. Christianity, which was in such contrast to Japanese culture at that time, introduced notions of human beings as individuals, a sense of equality, male and female chastity and purity - and these ideas began to germinate. This is clear even from Frois' *Bungohen*.

These ideas, however, had no sooner taken root than they were cut down. Such notions were a danger to those in power, a fact which did not escape their attention. For approximately three hundred years, during the period of national isolation when Christianity was banned and Japan was secluded from the world, the Tokugawa shogunate steered a unique course. The insular Japanese character formed during this period could be regarded as one reason for the friction with the present world.

For example, persecution of Christians and the following period of isolation can be linked to what are thought of as the ethical deficiencies of the nation as a whole. Such persecution occurred because of differences of faith, and Christians indisputably became victims of conscience. Japan has a history of having massacred nearly all the people who defended their faith with their lives. It is important to consider the grave serious significance of this, as author and minister Abe Mitsuko has written in the following.

> When I visited the sites of Christian martyrdom, I suddenly looked at the world we live in now and was aghast. We are caught in a whirlpool of bribery, corruption, and killing people for gratification.

There are people who even perjure and are proud of it. In trying to preserve the political power of their house, did not the Tokugawa shogunate root out from amongst our ancestors those who were genuinely concerned with their souls? What is it that we, the descendants of the persecutors of Christians and their collaborators, must learn from this history of martyrdom?[22]

Through reading history, I discovered among Christians in the sixteenth century, women whose lives I sympathised with and whose example I wanted to follow, and not only women, but also exceptional men too, such as Takayama Ukon, the Christian Daimyo. He was a rare man in not placing the values of bushido above all others, but displayed an awe for unseen, transcendental spiritual values, and discarded material possessions for the sake of that belief, even having the courage to offer life itself. It is comforting to know that there were such people in Japanese history. In this there is essentially no discrimination between men and women, because "in souls there is no sex." (William Penn).

The spiritual journey begun by Christians 450 years ago was, except for a handful of hidden Christians, broken during the period of national seclusion. Contemporary Christians should consciously reexamine this history and continue the journey, picking up from where it was broken off. This should not however, be construed as meaning that modern Christianity is equivalent to, or a continuation of Catholic orthodoxy. This is not my meaning at all and I should elucidate further.

It took a long time for me to finally meet the Christian women of 16th century Japan. As a woman I experienced conflict with the patriarchal system of the Christian Church, but after a period of darkness an encounter with Mary Daly's book *The Church and The Second Sex*[23] led me to a breakthrough. This book had sufficient academic substantiation regarding the tradition of the Christian Church and was the first clear formal objection from the inside by a

---

[22] Shinko to Ai to Shi to, Jinbutsu Nihon no Joseishi 7 Shueisha, Tokyo, 1977.

[23] Published 1968, my translation 1981.

woman. Western feminists have since begun to examine and criticise traditions one by one, with new eyes. Under this scrutiny the Judaeo-Christian patriarchal framework was exposed, but not rejected completely, the positive aspects that should be continued were recognised.

On further reflection about Japan, I found that the traditional religions of Shinto and Japanese-style Buddhism did not offer adequate salvation for me. Within the Christian tradition, those who had accepted Christianity ended up during the war becoming engulfed by the system. Of course there were a few exceptions, but not so much that I could consider it a tradition in which I could follow and live my life; I had misgivings about there being no tradition of women as role models and examples.

And then tracing back, I discovered the first Japanese women to come in contact with Christianity in the 16th century; people who did not forsake their faith, just a handful who became 'hidden Christians' and others who were massacred. Their example inspired me and gave a sense of continuity in a tradition. The fact that many of them did die in defense of their faith is not part of the Japanese idea of glorifying death, such as the Kamikaze Special Attack Forces did in World War II. I still do not know whether there was any group hysteria in the desire for a martyr's death and the world after death, but I do not believe it was simply an idealising of the fervent desire to go to heaven, what Marx called the religious opium.

The reason I would like to connect my life with those early Christian women, is because of the truth which shone through their lives, for which they would even sacrifice themselves if necessary. That truth is the love, equality and freedom as shown through the example of Jesus. In today's language we could call it human rights - something very far from belittling life and glorifying death. I think some of those early Christians thought that if this light were snatched away, or they were forced to reject it, then there was nothing left but to die. Those early Christians would emphatically reject the way of some present day Japanese to lie for personal gain and walk over other people without shame.

Feminism as one kind of cultural revolution questioned existing culture and, in a sense, caused destruction. After destruction however, a time of rebuilding must take place, but the question is where to start. In part it should begin with the search for roots and traditions - and I think it is now understood that this does not necessarily mean Catholic orthodoxy, maintaining the hierarchy as it does. For example, when I wrote that "... it was faith in a man called Jesus and his mother, a woman called Mary, was thus something more intimate, deeper and infinite," I was not saying that the Catholic Church's idolisation of Mary is worthy, regardless of Catholic or Protestant, it was a criticism of the very masculine bias of the concept of divinity in the Christian Church. Buddhism of the time also had a strong masculine bias, and Mary probably played a similar role to that of Kannon, the Goddess of Mercy, with her femininity being a comfort to women. But Mary is not a god, and her place is forever under the man with divine status.

It is clear from reading the Bible that Christianity sends a message of both liberation and oppression for women, a contradiction which is still not clearly recognised, and unfortunately when it is, ignorance is sometimes feigned.

The Conflict of Tradition and Modernity

Okuda Akiko

1. Introduction

Protestant Christianity came to Japan after the Meiji era had begun, bringing with it the concept of a sole transcendent God, which had a great impact on the values of the people who came in contact with it. In an age where polygamy was nothing out of the ordinary and women's rights were as good as non-existent, equality before god, the spirit of neighbourly love and charity, and a basic morality of male and female chastity based on a monotheistic faith, were revolutionary teachings for women in particular. Christianity's influence did not extend to the whole of society, however, and those who came in contact with it were limited mainly to a section of the middle class, but there were women whom it touched through education, or friends and acquaintances. How were they influenced by Christianity and were they emancipated by Christianity's perception of women, which ran counter to the prevailing Confucianist thinking outlined in *Onna Daigaku* (The Great Learning for Women, a widely used manual of behaviour and ethics)? If not, then why? These are questions I would like to examine.

It is generally accepted that Christianity's main impact on Japanese women was in the area of education. Certainly almost all women's educational institutions in the early part of the Meiji era were established by missionaries or people with Christian connections. The ban on Christianity, which had been treated as an heretical religion, was lifted in 1873 as a result of pressure from various foreign countries, but by that time a Miss Kidder had already opened a private school (later to become the Ferris School) at Yokohama in 1870 (Meiji 3), and mission schools were rapidly being established across the country. For example between 1870-77 (Meiji 3-10), Number 6A Girls School and eight other schools were established; 1878-81 (Meiji

11-14) Baika Girls School and 4 other schools; 1882-85 (Meiji 15-18) Toyo Eiwa and 3 other schools; and during the period of westernisation from 1886-90 (Meiji 19-23) Sanyo Girls School and some 26 other schools were established. Altogether, there were 45 mission schools built from the beginning of the Meiji period until Meiji 23.

Missionaries stressed the development of women's education because it was a means of proselytising, but also because it was a means of improving what was for them the surprisingly low status of women as compared to western countries. There were almost no government and municipal offices for women's eductional institutions. The government's westernisation policies also played a part in the spread of mission schools, together with women's fervent desire for education. Girls who studied at mission schools were middle-class and their numbers were limited, but the significance of their having the chance to receive an education equivalent to boy's, was great, and the level of education is said to have been quite high. Religious education also taught girls a new morality and to believe in monogamy. In an era where there was licensed prostitution and more than one wife per man was a generally accepted custom, such respect of women was a novel idea.

There is no detailed information available on the kinds of lives that each individual led after graduating from mission schools. Probably some assisted their husbands in mission work, and others such as Yajima Kajiko became involved in social movements and women's education. Or, there may have been women who unknown to others ran their household based on Christian principles and passed their faith on to the next generation. Even if many "were influenced by Christianity, there is scant possibility that it would be comprehended in the internal spritual structure of Japanese people,"[1] and after graduation it seems they passed their whole life indifferent to Christianity.

---

[1] Doi Akio, Nihon Purotesutanto Kurisutokyoshi, Shinkyo Shuppansha, Tokyo 1980.

But there were women, albeit few, who found a modern self through Christianity and moved one step further away from a traditional woman's way of life. In this paper I would like to examine the lives of two such women, Shimizu Shikin and Soma Kokko. I chose these two because they stand out amongst women of the Meiji Period, and because Christianity played a part in their self-development. They were also appealing women who led independent lives in their early years, but eventually compromised with the patriarchal family system after marraige and reverted to a more conventional lifestyle. Through their lives I would like to consider the conflict of tradition and modernity, and why Christianity was not able to emancipate women in a true sense.

2. Shimizu Shikin - Writer and Women's Rights Advocate

Shimizu Shikin was born as Shimizu Toyoko in 1868 (the first year of Meiji) in Okayama Prefecture. She studied at the Kyoto District First Girls School, and then at eighteen was married to a man chosen by her father, a lawyer named Okazaki Masaharu. Okazaki was active in the Freedom and People's Rights Movement, also known as the Popular Rights Movement, which was still going strong despite having passed its peak period of activity. Toyoko became deeply involved in the movement through her husband, even taking to the rostrum to speak all around the country. After three years, however, her marriage broke down. Her first work, "The Broken Ring" is said to be an autobiographical novel depicting the circumstances of her divorce. According to this novel, it seems that many men in the Rights Movement were feudal and despotic, casually taking lovers whilst believing that men should dominate women in the home.

The first-person narrator never takes her engagement ring off and wears it always with the jewel removed, because when she looks at the ring it brings back bitter sharp memories, and "thanks to the great suffering and grief this ring has given me, it brings out the spirit in me to become an independent person at last."

The era in which the novel is set was one when divorce had a very damaging impact on a womans reputation, but through the Popular Rights Movement Shikin had realised that "unfortunate misery does not always have to be woman's fate" and expresses the resolve to not be beaten by the stigma of divorce, moving away from a traditional lifestyle toward self-reliance. Nevertheless, she saw divorce as not just an individual tragedy but a problem for all women; "... without realising it, western women's theory has entered my head, and I have come to believe that Japanese women too must now achieve even a little of the happiness which is their natural right. One reason for this is to be diverted from ones own melancholy for a time, and another is the wish to save many women from the unhappiness of public opinion." After her divorce Shikin went to Tokyo and joined Iwamoto Zenji's pioneering women's magazine, *Jogaku Zasshi*, where she thrived as a journalist writing essays, critiques and interviews.

With the passing of the first flush of modernisation in the early part of the Meiji Period, the government began to feel threatened by the Popular Rights Movement and subsequently suppressed it. It was a time when there was a big shift of position aimed at securing a centralised state through the promulgation of the imperial mandate for establishing of the National Diet, and adoption of education policies based on Confucian ideas of family and morality. The Diet was established but women did not receive the right to vote; their political and social activities were prohibited by the 'Law of Assembly', and there was discussion of a proposed law prohibiting even listening to the House of Representatives.

Shikin wrote in response, "why is it that women are not permitted to listen to political assemblies?" In *Naite Aisuru Shimai ni Tsugu* (Cry of Appeal to my Beloved Sisters) she continued her protest; "without exception we twenty million women are turned into cripples", protesting vehemently that "boldly and without apology under the name of dividing male and female into wise and not wise, able and not able, any Tom Dick or Harry has the qualification to be soldiers, bear arms and participate in political assemblies, but women are not recognised as being capable of participating no matter how much of a genius she may be. What strange way of thinking is this?" she strongly protested. This assertion is reminiscent of "A Vindication of the Rights of Woman," written by English feminist Mary Wollstonecraft after the French Revolution, but at the time Shikin had not heard of Wollstonecraft. She probably learned much about the concept of women's rights through the Popular Rights Movement, and in particular from the ideas of Ueki Emori, with whom she was said to be good friends.

Ueki was an intellectual, political fighter, and central figure in the Freedom and People's Rights Movement. His ideas were apparently formed from Christianity and through reading translations of Rousseau, Spenser and others. He was a man of great insight, and perceived very early on the problems of the family system, believing that it must be reformed in order to accomplish democratisation of the nation. After becoming frustrated with the Popular Rights Movement, he returned to his hometown in Kochi Prefecture where he developed a critique of the patriarchal family system in a series of editorials in the local Sando Shimbun newspaper, under the titles of 'Parents and Children', 'Men, Women and Matrimony,' 'Hopes for Women of the World' and 'Japanese People and the Concept of the *Ie*.' He also wrote *Toyo no Fujo* (Eastern Women), for which Shikin wrote part of the preface, and *Fujin no Kenri* (Women's Rights).

Shikin's advocacy of women's rights, born as it was of experience, had a force that was lacking in Ueki's, who had only an intellectual comprehension of the concepts. Ueki advocated equality of spouses, women's right to participate in politics, inheritance rights, and was even active in the movement to abolish licensed prostitution on the basis that 'one man one wife' is a universal ethic. Yet there were contradictions between his ideas and his actions, and there was a period when he himself indulged in going to the red-light district.

Shikin's articles published in *Jogaku Zasshi*, 'How Prepared are Modern Women Students' and 'Hopes for Women's Education', also indicate a shift in her thinking beyond a simple advocation of women's political rights to a critique of the family system itself. The former article was aimed at women students wrappped in sweet dreams of marriage. "[Women students] think of marriage only as hope and happiness, a delightful peace that happens easily with nothing to worry about and nothing to be wary of. Similar to, for example, the trouble Eve unwittingly caused by singing near the snake."

And yet simply because of the high ideals attained through studying at girls schools, there were far more difficulties for women than in the past, as she wrote in the following: "Your future prospects indeed open out before you, but in the Japan of today there are many difficulties; whether it be in the home, or between husband and wife, there are many things which should be improved or changed and which must be resolved between twenty million sisters and twenty million brothers." She appealed to future generations of women, saying: "If you have reached this point [of marriage], it must be with the resolve of becoming a pioneer and reformer, and should the family of the man you find suitable have no desire to improve, you must still never go back on this resolution."

These lines were written when Shikin was greatly depressed after not only going through divorce, but also breaking off relations with Oi Kentaro, a comrade in the Popular Rights Movement, whom Shikin had thought held the same ideals. She received a double blow in learning that another woman in the movement, Kageyama (Fukuda) Hideko, was also Oi's lover and also gave birth to his child around the same time as Shikin. It was during this period when she was working at *Jogaku Zasshi* that she came in contact with Christianity.

Six years later in 'Hopes for Women's Education' (1896 [Meiji 29]), she criticised many intellectuals as too much wedded to only a "pretext of education for women," because although men are educated as human beings, "women are also human beings, but a thorough education for them is cast aside," the aim of their education being only to cultivate 'good wives and wise mothers.' At the time, debate over equal rights for men and women was gradually subsiding, and it was a period in which the groundwork for 'good wife, wise mother' education was steadily being laid. Shikin questioned why it was that men and women were divided, saying, "the spirit of much of women's education up to the present day, has been all the more convenient to cultivate women as they should be for men's purposes. There are some who would say, however, that mutual support and encouragement is not a lamentable thing in striving to be a good person and citizen. But it ought not be a happy thing for the nation that one half of the population are thus completely absorbed by the other half." Her discernment was sharp in asking why women are not human beings as well.

Although a Christian-based concept of human rights permeated her ideas at more than any other time up to then, she did not become baptised. While working at *Jogaku Zasshi* she was also the writing instructor at Meiji Girls' School and thus came to know many Christians, such as Meiji Girls' School Head and editor of *Jogaku Zasshi*, Iwamoto Zenji, also Uchimura Kanzo, Uemura Masahisa, and Kawai Shinsui, her most intimate friend amongst the editorial staff of *Jogaku Zasshi*.

In 1891 (Meiji 24), she sent the following letters to Kawai:

"As of last spring I have resolved on following the Christian path which I have been implicitly trained in."

"I have recently been gradually reading the Bible closely and giving it great thought; through the words and spirit of Christ, there is never a time when I am without hope and peace of mind can be found ... even the profoundly sinful are received as God's children ... sometimes the question emerges causing my sister distress, but she has at length resolved on becoming a Christian ..."

"... the situation is so complex I cannot put it into words truly, the guidance of various teachers and God's teachings since last spring ... thrown in a kind of non-confining prison as punishment for desiring to enter the gate of the lord and thoughtlessly failing to catch Christ's words ... it is my sister who progresses and the spiritual route taken must be different ..."

These letters appear to show that even if she did not profess to be a believer, Shikin had deeply accepted Christianity. The child she had by Oi was being looked after at her family's home. Unmarried mothers were regarded harshly in public opinion, but Shikin accepted this as a trial from God. Fukuda Hideko condemned Shikin in her autobiography, *Warawa no Hanshogai* (Half My Life, 1904), but in contrast to Hideko's deep-seated grudge, Shikin never once said anything which sounded like an excuse for herself. Recognising her own mistakes as such, living with that guilt and bearing bitterness against no one, Shikin could be said to be more of a Christian than those who professed themselves to be believers.

Letters to Shikin from Kozai Yoshinao in later days inquire as to "the reasons for your believing in Christianity and why you desire to believe," so it can be inferred that for at least one period Shikin was earnest in putting Christianity at the center of her life.

An acceptance of Christianity is at least one factor in explaining why she could give up writing. Shikin exhibited talent in her essays and novels and a great deal was expected of her in the future, but after meeting and marrying Kozai Yoshinao she gracefully abandoned her pen at his request. Yoshinao's proposing to marry a woman with a history of divorce who had also borne a child as the mistress of Oi Kentaro, and holding her in esteem despite her past, made him an unusual man for the times. Their married life was a happy one it seems, and according to her sons a democratic atmosphere reigned where even in old age their parents debated like students. Yoshinao was a scholar of praiseworthy achievements who became the president of Tokyo University, and the sons were also excellent achievers. From the public's point of view, it was a fulfilling life as a wife and mother.

But how was it as an individual woman? Shikin had written a great deal in ten years, had talent and understood well the situation women were placed in; there would have been much she wanted to pass on to women of the time. No matter how democratic relations with her husband may have been, it could not have compensated for her having to abandon all ambition. This is not democratic at all. Are not equal relations those in which each helps the other person to realise their ambitions.

Sometimes "the tears gather and we quarrelled." These words were probably an expression of resentment at having to shut out herself to lead life as a wife and mother. Compared to English feminist Mary Wollstonecraft, who lived a hundred years before Shikin and continued writing until her death although constrained in the same way, Japanese women living in the Meiji era must seem locked in the dark ages. If Shikin had not ceased writing and continued to expound her ideas, then Hiratsuka Raicho and other feminists of the next generation would have inherited them and undoubtedly feminism in Japan would have bloomed a lot earlier.

Murakami Nobuhiko, a well-known women's historian, writes about Shikin in *Meiji Joseishi* (History of Meiji Women), highly evaluating the goodness of her husband, Kozai Yoshinao, and their union, and imagining that Shikin led a happy life unbowed by her past. Yoshinao certainly showed courage in acting according to his conscience as a scholar and not yielding to threats when involved in the survey of pollution of the Watarasegawa river by ore from the Ashio Copper Mine, but at home although he was a tolerant man who respected hs wife, he also behaved in a manner common amongst Japanese men, like a child wanting to be spoilt by their wife. However superior a scholar, and rare and great a man he was, the fact that it was still necessary to be cared for by his wife like a child, is from a woman's point of view an egotisitcal attitude.

The only time in her marriage when Shikin was actually able to write and produce several books, is when her husband went to Europe for five years to study. One of the books from this period was an enterprising novel about burakumin victims of discrimination, called *Imin Gakuen* (Immigrants School) written much earlier than Shimazaki Toson's book on the same topic, *Hakai* (The Broken Commandment). Throughout her life she maintained an interest in social and womens issues, attested to by an entry in her diary of 1915 found after her death, where she joyfully noted that the universal suffrage movement had expanded to each region of the country. She also was not remiss about reading and continued into her old age, reading for two hours until late at night after finishing the housework, saying, "this is my only free time." After reading novels by Sata Ineko and Nakajo Yuriko, she was overjoyed that "at last good novels by women have begun to appear again."

Some of her ideas were passed on through her husband and sons, but to later generations it seems that Shikin still had the desire to pursue her own ambitions after marriage, even given the restrictions of the times. I think she wanted to live for herself more than for her husband and sons, and pass on many things to future generations of women.

3. Soma Kokko - From Christianity to Buddhism

Usui Yoshimi has already written a monumental work on the life of Soma Kokko, *Azumino*, but here I would like to focus discussion on her beliefs. Soma Kokko was born as Hoshi Ryo in Sendai in 1896 (Meiji 9), the fourth daughter of Hoshi Kishiro and Minoji in a samurai family come down in the world. She grew up in a religious environment with people such as her aunt the feminist, Sasaki Toyoju, a devout Christian and secretary of the Christian Women's Temperance Society in Japan. Amongst her relatives there were also Catholic believers and a Greek Orthodox Church Priest. From around twelve years of age she began to attend Sunday School and at fourteen was baptised by Oshikawa Masayoshi. At sixteen she entered a mission school for girls in Miyagi prefecture, but left school in sympathy with a friend who was expelled for planning a strike, and transferred to the Ferris Girl's school in Yokohama when she was eighteen.

The time at which she came in contact with Christianity in Sendai was the so-called 'Age of Westernisation' and was an era in which the influence of Christianity spread markedly. This can be seen in the increase of churches and followers; at the end of 1878 (Meiji 11), there were 44 churches and 1,600 followers across the country but by 1985 (Meiji 18), there were 160 churches and 11,000 followers, and in 1886 there were 193 churches and 13,000 followers, in 1888 there were 206 churches and 23,000 followers, and in 1890 it had increased to 300 churches and 34,000 followers. Many of society's elite flocked to church, and applications to mission schools poured in.

Mission schools, including the Ferris School which Ryo entered, were considered highly attractive by young girls of the Meiji period, as Matsumiya Kazuya wrote in the following:

"The pleasure of contact with foreign missionaries, hearing about unusual foreign countries, becoming wide-eyed at fashions in foreign magazines, a pride in learning English - the mission school was the spring of a fount of knowledge, and a place where vogues were born. Ribbons in place of hairpins, shoes instead of geta, showing the tip of red inner sleeves inside brown hakama, walking jauntily with English book in one hand and a western umbrella in the other - 'mission girls' were colorful figures of the times."[2]

But this school could not meet her requirements; Ryo was interested in literature and was not satisfied with the stern moralistic Christian education, so she moved again to Iwamoto Zenji's Meiji Girls School.

The Meiji Girls' School was a school run on Christian principles but not by missionaries. It was established in 1885 (Meiji 18) by Kimura Kumaji, whose wife Toko was school head during the early years. Iwamoto Zenji became head after Toko died of an illness. Unlike the Ferris school, the buildings were humble, and the desks and chairs were rickety, but it had a fascination for young women, as Kokko writes:

"Progressive and artistic education, and the head, Iwamoto Zenji's meteoric existence in the world of education, continue to amaze the eyes and ears of intelligent people; as well as his wife Wakamatsu Shizuko, famous for her brilliant translations. How could these two be described? Accomplished, up to date and informed, as poets, or thinkers - whatever words are chosen they are not sufficient to describe the genius of these two ...... it is no wonder that young girls flocked to the Meiji School with a religious passion."[3]

Iwamoto Zenji gathered around him as teachers young literary graduates of Meiji Gakuin University, writers in their twenties

---

[2] Nihon Kurisutokyo Shakai Bunkashi, Shinkigensha, 1948.

[3] Mokui, Soma Aizo, Kokko Chosakushu, Nihonjin no Jiten 6, Heibonsha, Tokyo 1980.

representative of Meiji Romanticism such as Togawa Shukotsu, Baba Kocho, and Shimazaki Toson. A number of platonic relationships were said to have developed between the young teachers and their young students.

After graduating from Meiji Girl's School, Ryo married Soma Aizo in 1897 (Meiji 30), with the encouragement of a religious instructor. Ryo was 22 and Aizo was 27 years old. Aizo was a Christian from East Hotaka village in Shinshu (Nagano prefecture), from an old family which up to his grandfather's generation had served as the village head and bore other signs of distinction, such as having a family surname (rare up until the Meiji era) and being permitted to wear a sword. The head of the family was Aizo's oldest brother, Yasubei, who was like a father to him because their parents had died when Aizo was only an infant. Aizo graduated from Matsumoto Middle School and entered the Tokyo Semmon Gakko (which later became Waseda University), during which time he began to attend church and was baptised. After graduating he returned home and while working at sericulture, engaged in mission work, organised a temperance society and was also active as a young district guidance counsellor. The temperance society was formed not just for the purpose of reforming the village people's drinking habits, but also for moral and self-improvement. There were night classes to educate the village youth, with influential leaders in the church such as Uchimura Kanzo and Uemura Masahisa sometimes invited to come and give lectures. It was the members of Aizo's temperance society who strove to open a private school called Kensei Gijuku when Iguchi Kigenji was rejected by the public schools. Aizo and the young members gathered every night, not just to talk about problems of farming and the village, but also for ardent debates about a Christian's mission and faith.

Ryo began her life as a bride in the house of her brother-in-law, in this country village in Shinshu. The following year a daughter, Toshi, was born and two years after that a son, Yasuo. She was a colourful figure, debating with Aizo's circle on an equal footing, decorating a tree at Christmas and playing the organ, but as a country wife, Ryo, who was brought up in the city, could not do even do half a persons work let alone one, and the realities of country life were much harsher than she had imagined. An essay entitled *Nanji, Inaka Yo* (Hey You - This is the Country), sent by her to *Jogaku Zasshi* around this time, frankly depicts the harsh working life of an agricultural village and her feelings of alienation and defeat during this period.

After four years of living in Hotaka the couple eventually resolved to leave the village on the pretext of a change of climate for Ryo, who suffered from asthma, but the conditions for their going were to leave their daughter Toshi behind in the Soma *ie*, like a hostage. Caught between her desire to leave the country and distress at having to sacrifice her daughter, Kokko eventually put herelf first, but felt guilty about her daughter for the rest of her life.

In Tokyo the couple opened a small bread shop and gradually increased their regular customers through hard work and ingenuity. After a few years they made a successful move to Shinjuku where they named their business Nakamuraya. Their policy was to sell good quality products cheaply, establish relationships on an equal footing between owners and employees, and to conduct business in a dignified manner without discounting. Such a concept is similar to the protestant work ethic of working diligently for the glory of God. The nature of their work made cooperation essential for success, but the two were on equal terms even apart from work. If anything, it was essentially Ryo who kept the shop going while Aizo returned to the village for a few months every year to attend to his sericulture. If Ryo were not there, unyielding, undistractcd and carrying out their plans, the business probably would not have succeeded. Nevertheless, it was Aizo's job to raise funds and make future plans, and in that sense the wife had to follow the husband's lead.

As the business expanded, various people collected around the Somas. Amongst them were artists such as sculptor Ogiwara Rokuzan (Morie), painter Nakamura Tsune, Tobari Kogan, Yanagi Keisuke, poet and sculptor Takamura Kotaro, and other colourful people such as Akita Ujaku, Kamichika Ichiko and the Russian poet Vasili Iakovlevich Eroshenko. These artistic activities of the Nakamuraya salon, as it was called, were largely sustained by Ryo who was a good mixer, liked helping people and had an artistic bent having been a literary enthusiast in her youth. The relationship between Ryo, Ogiwara, Nakamura and also young Waseda University scholar Katsurai Tonosuke, however, was more than just a simple relationship between a salon mistress and regular frequenters it seems. The salon was also well-known for sheltering Indian independence activist and patriot Subhas Chandra Bose, who was under an expulsion order from the Japanese government.

After coming to Tokyo and being pressed with the demands of running a business, raising children and looking after the people who turned to her for help, Ryo did not go to church and became indifferent to Christianity, but it was not as if she had lost her religious spirit. By her late thirties life had become somewhat more settled both physically and mentally, and she began to go to Okada Torajiro's meditation training because of bad health amongst other things. At fifty her daughter Toshi died, and together with Aizo she formally converted to Buddhism through the teaching of Jodo Sect priest Watanabe Kaikiyoku. In her leaning towards Buddhism there probably lay a sense of guilt at having sacrificed her daughter Toshi to her own egoism. Toshi had married Bose and moved many times while fleeing from the authorities, until eventually she died from worry and care at the young age of twenty eight. Ryo was the one who had encouraged her to marry Bose in order to protect his safety, and this probably added to the guilt she felt about her daughter.

It was also a shock for Ryo to discover that her husband, who participated in the anti-licensed prostitution movement and who she trusted as a Christian to believe in monogamy, had what was known as a 'hometown wife.' For Ryo, who had attended church since a young girl, the 'purity, righteousness and beauty' that she had been taught by Christianity to believe in, was besmirched. She had borne 5 boys and 4 girls by Aizo and could not forgive his infidelity. But although she could not forgive him, she did not confront her husband directly and the festering thought manifested itself in her bad mental and physical shape. Later she would reminisce that "when once having opened my eyes to the deep recesses of the heart, and reflecting on the inner life, there are truly so many things that ought to be repented," a penitence which included various thoughts it appears.

But why did Ryo turn to Buddhism? Takeda Kiyoko has conjectured that it is likely that the ascetic faith taught by Protestantism was too severe for Ryo, and what she desired was a more merciful faith which accepted oneself as one is and consoled the heart's pain, not the severe kind of Christianity taught by Iguchi Kigenji.[4] Unlike Iguchi, the narrow-minded, militant Calvinist and so-called moral 'saint of Hotaka', the teacher she studied under, Okada Torajiro, and Jodo sect priest Watanabe Kaikyoku, were open and broad-minded people on a different scale.

The particularly ascetic nature of Protestantism in Japan is due to the evangelical nature of Christianity brought to the country from the west during the Meiji era, and also to the fact that many of the people who accepted Christianity at this time and became leaders of the church, were former samurai. These were samurai who had been shut out by the Satsuma and Choshu military alliance during the Meiji revolution, and had had to abandon ambitions to govern as saviours of the people. Their sense of responsibility to reform society was thus transformed into devotion as Christians, and the old samurai consciousness was merely maintained unchanged in the guise of the conscience of the new social leaders. Hence Christianity became much more ascetic in Japan than other countries.

However, if it is as Takeda says, that Kokko sought such tolerance from religion, this is still not reason enough to turn from Christianity to Buddhism; Christianity is also supposed to be a religion to help those who are troubled. The deeper reason lies in the nature of the people who accepted Christianity. Kokko was baptised at only fourteen years of age, and seems to have continued with this faith of her girlhood without ever experiencing any spiritual crisis which would cause her to reaffirm her beliefs. The way in which Christianity was accepted and absorbed in Japan has much to do with this.

---

[4] Takeda Kiyoko, Seito to Itan no Aida, Tokyo Daigaku Shuppankai, Tokyo 1976.

According to research by Sugii Rokuro, which analsyed people who had maintained faith for the approximately thirty years from 1888 (Meiji 21) until 1921 (Taisho 10), there are three patterns of acceptance amongst converts; direct, refracted and compound. The direct type were those who found sympathy with Christian principles of equality and humanism through their English education, or who came to believe though contact with missionaries and their credos of faith. The refractory type came to believe by experiencing loneliness and grief through the loss of relatives for example, and the compound type were a combination of the previous two. Many of those who could be classified refractory, were conversions as a result of physical failure or loss, and there were extremely few conversions through spiritual questioning.[5] The direct type were overwhelmingly numerous amongst Japanese believers.

For women in particular, the peak ages for conversion were at 16 years and 26 years; after school education had finished at the earliest, and four or five years after marriage in the late cases. In short, it was common for them to become Christians because of their mission school education or through their husband's influence. There are very few conversions in the age group below this, and an overwhelming number of conversions occurred after the husband was first baptised and followed later by the wife. Based on these facts, Sugii concluded that even in Christian households where the old commonly accepted concept of community structure was sloughed off through belief in this new faith, subordination of the wife to the husband was still alive and well.

Of the three, Kokko is a typical direct type. She did not experience any spiritual or philosophical crisis, and also did not arrive at her faith through reading the Bible by herself and finding the way to God. Her understanding of Christianity was derived from people such as Iwamoto Zenji and Iguchi Kigenji, and her reasons for entering Meiji Jogako were because of an interest in literature, not religion. For these

---

5   Sugii Rokuro, Meijiki Kurisutokyo no Kenkyu, Dohosha, Kyoto 1984.

reasons disillusionment with living people could easily translate to disillusionment with her faith.

4. Christianity and the Family System

Both Shikin and Kokko were surprisingly independent for women of the Meiji era. Yet why is it that once married, even they submitted to tradition, with the wife subordinate to the husband. Why was Christianity of no help in their emancipation?

The first reason that comes to mind is the firm grip of the patriarchal family system holding women in their place. The twenties and thirties of the Meiji era when Shikin and Kokko encountered Christianity and thought of emancipation, was also the period when the Confucian principle of 'good wife, wise mother' was adopted as an education policy and the infrastructure for such education was established. This movement began during the second decade of the Meiji period, but there was a more definite framework after the Regulations for Girls's High Schools were issued in 1895 (Meiji 28), which set out an educational policy of teaching such virtuous things for girls as housework, sewing and filial piety. In the Directive on Girls' High Schools issued in 1899 (Meiji 32), the fostering of good wives and wise mothers was established as the basic policy for girls education. The Sino-Japanese war of 1894-95 had taught the government the necessity of improving women's education and cultivating a sense of family for national strength, and the way to do this was to regard the country as one family by creating the concept of a 'family nation' which integrates loyalty and fidelity, and expanding the patriarchal family system of the samurai class to the entire populace; policies that were strengthened by law.

This directive also had a great influence on Christian girls' schools, as those schools which taught religion and conducted religious ceremonies were no longer able to call themselves high schools. The number of entrants declined dramatically when teachers' qualifications gained there were not recognised and top-grade schools would not accept graduates' entrance qualifications, as they did for state girls' high schools. This decline reached a peak in Meiji 23, when the steady decrease in applicants to mission schools threatened some with closure. Not only were mission schools discriminated against in this way, but readings of the Imperial Rescript on Education were compulsory and there was government interference in religious education.

The second reason that Christianity did not aid in women's emancipation is the fact that there was never any confrontation between Christianity and the patriarchal family system. In areas where there could have been dispute, the Christian Church took the postion, if anything, of vindicating the patriarchal family system. The sole object of many Christians was to eradicate polygamy, and they overlooked the role of the patriarchal family system as a basic unit supporting the Emperor system. The 'White Paper on One Husband One Wife' submitted to elder statesmen by the Christian Women's Temperance Society in June 1889 (Meiji 22), reveals how maintaining the family system was regarded as important, as the following extract illustrates:

I. Whereas in the middle and upper echelon homes in our country, the practice of keeping a mistress is rampant. The evils arising from keeping a mistress are:

Number one; a husband maltreats his wife and the household becomes grieved ending with the husband and wife living apart.

Number two; omitted

Number three; mistresses desire to steal those household effects, and desire their children to become head of the family, which will end in extermination of the family.

Number four; omitted

Number five; with one family as the base of the one country, the effects of the unhappy tumult of one family will extend to the nation.

Therefore, they maintained, Christianity was the only means to realise the one husband one wife system.

I: The first step for the salvation of one husband many wives, is through the Christian Church. Confucianism has not the moral vigor, besides its teachings hold mistresses in contempt. Buddhism views women as sinners, and if even amongst devout followers of Buddha and high priests, there are many with more than one wife, it is because it is suffice to only request it. Advocation of one husband one wife by the Christian church will certainly render it possible.

Monogamy certainly represents progress, but even so women's subordinate position will not change while the family head has absolute authority and there are no grounds on which men and women can become equal. The important thing is the recognition that it is the system of patriarchy itself which oppresses women, not individual men. In a patriarchal society where the division of labor according to sex is taken for granted, whatever democratic ideas of equality a husband like Kozai Yoshinao for example, may have held, there can only be equality within the framework of a sexual division of labor, and consequently as a wife Shikin was not able to pursue her ambitions.

The systematic theorisation of the family systems obstruction of women's emancipation is however, quite recent; before that individual women could only confront the system by themselves. This was an almost impossible task in an era in which the patriarchal family system was so strongly established. Even Shikin, who protested so strongly against the 'good wife, wise mother' ideology, eventually quashed her own ambitions to lead a life as a good wife supporting her husband; and Kokko, who seemed independent and was an equal working partner with her husband, did not confront him with his infidelity but instead sought salvation in Buddhism because of the various anguishes, which had their basis in the family system.

The strengthening of the patriarchal system in post-industrial revolution Europe, is also an example of how a system of gender control supporting from below, and the patriarchal family system, were necessary for the expansion of capitalism. In the case of Europe, the Christian church played a large role in strengthening the patriarchal family system, but in Japan where religion is not as influential, it was education which took on that role. The success of this during the twenties and thirties of the Meiji era has already been described, and the Christian church, which also seemed to teach women a new way of living, was no different in its promotion of the 'good wife, wise mother' ethic. The prospectus, for example, of the Shizuoka Eiwa Girls Mission School established in 1887 states:

"The man and woman couple forms the basis of the home ...... girls ought not only to become wives but also mothers, and it is mothers of course who have a profound influence over those girls .... the importance of improving character through the education of girls ought to be remembered."

These were the admirable objectives of 'good wife wise mother' education, and as can be seen from this prospectus, the school being a Christian one did not make much difference. Such perceptions of women were commonly held by almost all Christian leaders and educators.

Many Christian leaders of the time viewed western women who took responsibility for housekeeping and children's education, as exemplifying the ideals of womanhood, and American middle-class wives in particular were regarded as such, but the distinction between this ideal and the 'good wife, wise mother' that the Meiji administrators desired, was ambiguous. In actual fact the middle-class American women they saw as a model from the end of the eighteenth century until the beginning of the nineteenth century, were never equal citizens with men because of the self-restraining qualities of piety, purity, obedience and self-sacrifice promoted by the clergy and internalised during the Victorian era.

The third possible reason for Christianity's failure to aid in the emancipation of women is, as already stated, the evangelical nature of Protestantism which stressed human sin in the Meiji era. For Japanese people who did not have a concept of a single transcendent God, however, it was very difficult to comprehend such issues as original sin and Christ's expiation of sin. There were missionaries who said the Japanese were a "light-hearted" people and few of them "lamented greatly over their sins." Because of this, Christian leaders' (though not all of course) understanding of Christianity was slanted both ethically and morally.

Well-known wrtier and critic Kamei Katsuichiro identifies lack of pleasure, stoicism and dogmatism as three similarities between Christianity and communism,[6] tendencies which are evident in Christianity in Japan not only during the Meiji era, but also today.

Although Shikin and Kokko both had a different understanding of Christianity, they did have in common the tendency of Christians for self-judgement. Their lives would have been much different if they had managed to extract from Christianity an understanding that one does not have to suffer, that the frank pursuit of ambition is acceptable, and that physical emancipation as well as spiritual emancipation is important, with the two being indivisible. With such an understanding perhaps Kokko, who fascinated many men, had a strong sense of self and was brimming with pioneering spirit, could have led a bolder kind of life like the poet and feminist writer Yosano Akiko. Shikin might have opposed her husband and spurned self-sacrifice to start writing again and leave a name for herself as a feminist, but then her husband would not have become head of Tokyo University.

Christianity in the Meiji era did go some way toward raising the status of women, but it did not become a vehicle for their emancipation. If anything, those who showed the most severe opposition on the occasion of the appearance of Hiratsuka Raicho's 'new woman', were Christian households and those belonging to the intelligentsia,[7] who were inclined towards preservation of the order more than the emancipation of women.

The oppression of women by religion, including Christianity, has a long history. Can religion really contribute to women's emancipation in Japan? This is a question which has still to be answered. If it can, this will come in the wake of a feminist critique of religion, something which only became possible in the west after the seventies with the

---

6 Kamei Katsuichiro in Gendai Nihon Kurisutokyo, ed. Kuyama Yasushi, Sobunsha, Tokyo, 1961.
7 Soron - Atarashii Onna Izen in Meiji no Onna, ed. Kida Junichiro, Vol. 9, Sanichi Shobo, Tokyo, 1969.

advent of feminist theologians who believed that Christianity and women's emancipation are connected. In Japan this process has, at last, only just begun.

Women's Role - A Channel for Power

Igeta Midori

1. Rationing of Ambition by the State

In 1867 the Tokugawa shogunate collapsed, leaving the new Meiji administration to face various domestic and foreign crises in the ensuing political and economic chaos, and also with the threat of continuing colonisation of Asia by Western powers. To counter these problems the administration set out to accrue sufficient national capital and military strength befitting a wealthy and powerful modern state which would be recognised by the great Western powers. Introducing western technology and culture, and modernising industry and the military therefore became a priority. The framework within which the government chose to pursue this modernisation was a powerful centralised political rule, necessitating the creation of such a national consciousness as would enable the nation to submit to such governance. Hence in order to foster such a consciousness, the reign over the nation by an emperor descended from the gods and of pure lineage, was legitimised in the name of restoring imperial rule. Fears that western science and culture would have a divisive influence on Japanese cultural and spiritual unity led to the adoption of Shinto as a state religion, forcing the people to revere and submit to the mythical and religious authority of the Emperor.

The power to map out the course of the nation and shape public values to focus on industry and the military during this period, was in the hands of a small, male elite. Women, and men with no political or economic power, were expressly excluded from the centre of public values, having no choice but to submit to elite rule and conform to the system created by the government.

How was this rule received? Was it accepted reluctantly out of fear? The administration could have employed violence as punitive measures to enforce a reign of terror, but this would have been counter-productive. To establish a stable relationship with the majority and effectively utilise their labour, productive capacity and strength for protection against enemies of the political and economic system, it is more effective to foster the will for people to submit to the administration's authority of their own volition. This is, in effect, is what the Meiji administration set out to accomplish.

Not everyone was compliant, however, and there were some who opposed the official order; socialists, for example, who planned to put into practice ideas regarded as contravening the state system. On the whole, however, the majority of subjects were obedient. Against the background of the large scale foreign aggressions of the Sino-Japanese War, Russo-Japanese War, First World War and lead-up to the Pacific War, compulsory education and a higher education system were implemented as a means of integrating people into the hierarchical structure of state authority, and Japan was gradually and successfully moulded into an imperial nation.

The system of determining social status according to birth and descent was abolished under the slogan of 'Four Equal Classes,' and theoretically it became possible for all men to become part of the elite through their own efforts and ability. Although many were frustrated in their attempts by various difficulties, it became very clear that there was a desire to rise up the ladder from the ruled, to ruling class. A route to power had opened up. Rather than regarding this as a completely new innovation, it ought perhaps be seen as the administration simply giving a definite shape and aim to ambitions and raw energy already long latent amongst the ruled class. In any case, once subject to such ambitions, men became integrated into the hierarchical structure of state authority.

2. A Man's Ie - The Power of the Head of the House

The situation for women, on the other hand, was somewhat different. Women also desire authority in the sense of having power to exert influence over others, regulate their own situation and improve their lot, but in Meiji society they were completely excluded from the realm of public authority. Unlike men, there was no path along which they could channel an ambition for public authority. Nevertheless, women who also desired to enter the hierarchy of authority in the same way as men, did begin to emerge, but they were never encouraged, and there was little or no social acceptance of such ambition in women. But even if the kind of public authority held by men was not attainable, modern Japan did give women the possibility for securing a different kind of authority, within the *ie* (household) system, reorganised and reconstructed by the Meiji administration as a means of exercising control over the nation.

The precise origins of the *ie* system are not yet clear, but it is thought to have developed in samurai society around the end of the Muromachi era, when "a consciousness that an *ie* is something eternal, greater than individual family members, crossing over generations," was born, and the *kamei* (family name) was believed to represent the *ie*."[1] The person who inherited the family, the *katoku* (family head), was responsible for managing the family. Succession of males to the position of *katoku* and inheritance through the male line became stronger during the Sengoku (Warring States) period, when fighting ability was of great importance and men were highly regarded. A simple system of inheritance, adopted to prevent the dispersion of territory and subsequent weakening of *ie* power, markedly strengthened the authority of the *katoku* over family members. During the Edo bakuhan regime, there was systematic reorganisation of the social, economic and political order, with the *ie* as the basis, and thus *ie* ideology became refined. By the mid-Edo era, this ideology was generally accepted amongst wealthy land-owning farmers, merchant households with inheritable assets, and common people.

The *ie* became the core of rule and order in society. Samurais' daughters were denied the right to inherit family headship or wealth and were expected to marry into another *ie* to ensure the prosperity of their fathers' and brothers' *ie*, provide an heir to ensure the

---

[1] Otake Hideo, 'Ie' to Josei no Rekishi, Kobundo, 1977.

perpetutation of their husbands' family line, and competently manage household affairs.

With the exception of those who worked in the feudal lord's castle, women of the samurai class were not entitled to a retainers stipend, and were supported by fathers and brothers, or husbands and children after marriage. Women were regarded as perverse and innately stupid, and were supposed to always obey the commands and rule of the man who was the family head. But amongst the common classes, apart from upper-class farmers and merchants, women were recognised as contributing equally with men to the *ie*, working in the house as daughter, wife or mother, and compared to women of the samurai class, could act more independently.[2]

3. The Ie as an Ancestor Worship Group

The *ie* system is thought to have spread amongst the common classes from the mid-eighteenth century onwards. As a system, the *ie* became not only a "basic unit of life security"[3] and unit of the social structure supporting industry and the military, but also a religious group linking generations in the worship of their ancestors and a symbol of perpetuity. In this sense, the *ie* has a very strong religous aspect. Nakano Takashi defines the *ie* as follows: "taking the form of the latter early modern *ie* as a prototype, the reorganised form of the *ie* was a management body continually carrying out the indivisible labour of housework and family business with the object of developing and perpetuating the *ie* over generations, concentrating the members'

---

2 It was not simply that women were oppressed, in any period there were always women who resisted oppression and demonstrated the strength to secure freedom. Nevertheless, when arguing the freedom of women from the non-wealthy common class of premodern society, the social context should not be minimized as their freedom was restricted according to status and class, and the public arena was also structured according to the ideology of men's superiority.

3 Komoto Mitsugi, 'Ie' no Henshitsu to Senzo Saishi in Kingendai ni Okeru 'Ie' no Henshitsu to Shukyo, ed. Morioka Kiyomi, Shinchi Shobo, 1986.

labour to manage the family business, finances, and run the household while worshipping their ancestors, and encouraged by the belief that in so working for the family they would be rewarded with life after death." The authority of the family head to control all family matters, represent all family members, and be reponsible for the management of housework and business essential to achieving the family's aims, is recognised by all.[4]

The Meiji administration tried to instill a consciousness of the *ie* in people's minds by implementing laws, institutions, and compulsory education, which they furthermore attempted to unify with the idea that the state is an *ie* in which the Emperor is the parent of all his subjects. The *koseki* (household register) system was established in the interests of creating such a centralised unified state to enable comprehensive tax collection, military conscription and compulsory education. Under this system a family was defined as a group of relatives sharing the same *koseki* and household head. In the Meiji Civil Code enacted in 1898 (Meiji 31), the householder gained the right to decide where the family should live, and the householder's consent also became necessary for family members to marry if under the age of thirty for men, and twenty five for women. The person who inherited the postion of householder and incumbent authority, also inherited the privileges of lineage, including rights to religous implements and the family grave. In principle, the successor to family headship had to be a lineal descendant, with males, legitimate children and elders having priority and, as a result, inheritance by the eldest son became the norm.[5]

The French jurist G.E. Boissonade de Fontarabie was originally asked to be a member of the drafting committee for the new civil code which the government wanted to draw up in reponse to the major western powers' demands that Japan establish a modern legal system,

---

4 Nakano Takashi, Nihon no Kazoku in Kazoku no Bunkashi - Samazamana Katachi to Henka, edited by Hara Hiroko, Kobundo, 1986.

5 It was recognized that women could also be householders, but because basic thinking was that "men should naturally inherit the *ie*," this was treated as irregular.

and Japan's own desire to revise the so-called Unequal Treaties concluded during the 1850s and 1860s. The draft which Boissonade was instrumental in preparing, however, was designed to alter conventions of Japanese society with western ideas of modern citizenship; married couples would constitute the family nucleus instead of parent and child, and husband and wife would have equal rights and resposibilities. As such it was not adopted because it was thought "contrary to the beautiful tradition of Japan." Another draft, the Meiji Civil Code, was subsequently composed in which the authority of the householder was strengthened, but there was firm resistance to the enactment of a civil code itself from jurists such as Hozumi Yatsuka, who argued that "loyalty would disappear on the advent of a civil code." Hozumi saw Japan as a "country of ancestor worship," and maintained that "the source of the patriarch's authority is in the ancestors spirits, and the household gods that protect the family should have the authority to pass judgement on people belonging to the family. The idea that descendants must be obedient to their ancestors' spirits ought to be transmitted to the present representative of the family." Also, "considering we are a nation of people united by common ancestors, the people shall be obedient to the spirits of their ancestors, and receive life under their protection. The spirits of our ancestors reside in the Imperial Throne." Thus he argued the unity of the *ie* and the state, on the basis that the Japanese people originated from the Emperor's ancestors and are racially homogeneous.

Male and female equality based on modern civil rights was also advocated, but enforcement of the civil code was delayed, and in the end the Meiji Civil Code which passed through the Imperial Diet was one which largely incorporated old samurai customs and the concept of the *ie*. Although the *ie* was not directly stipulated in the articles on consanguinity and inheritance, unequal relations of the sexes were made very clear. For example, only adultery on the part of the wife could become a reason for divorce, the wife lost her legal capacity in transactions involving property, and the parental rights of mothers over their children were not recognised.

It should be noted, however, that even in advanced western nations at the time, the father's rights were powerful, and husbands and wives did not have equal rights under the law. This "shows the patriarchal nature of modern civil society, but in addition to this the Japanese Civil Code included the concept of the *ie* as the basis of support for the Emperor system; which in pre-war Japan defined the family and women's position within the family."[6]

4. The Meiji Ie and Women's Duties

The Emperor issued the Imperial Rescript on Education at the request of the government, which wanted to establish authority and legitimise education by the state. This imperial rescript commanded the Emperor's subjects to respect the constitution and obey the law at all times, to volunteer in case of emergency, and to support imperial prosperity forever; in other words the object of education was to cultivate loyal subjects who would fight for the emperor. The rescript exhorts filial piety, harmony between brothers and sisters, and concord between married couples, however filial piety and preserving the order of the *ie* were linked with loyalty to the emperor, and equal relations between the sexes or husband and wife were never assumed. Primary school textbooks were written in order to teach morals and foster a spirit of patriotism and reverence for the emperor in accordance with the direction of the imperial rescript. The textbooks instructed girls to be obedient and gentle, and learn sewing and cooking, because "girls will go to someone else's house when they are grown, to obey their husband, serve their parents-in-law, and manage matters inside the home." It also stated that "the husband is responsible for outside affairs, and the wife takes care of matters inside the home." This was the division of labour for married couples. Outside affairs meant jobs such as warrior, farmer, artisan or merchant, the four classes into

---

[6] Nagahara Kazuko, Tennosei to Ie in Nihon Josei no Rekishi - Sei, Ai, Kazoku, Sogo Joseishi Kokyukaihen, Kadokawa Shoten, Tokyo, 1992.

which Japanese people were divided until the Edo period, but officially abolished after the Meiji Restoration. Matters inside the home meant "carrying out morning and evening chores, sewing clothes, and education of infant children." It states that a woman's role and duty was to become a good wife and mother, and to protect her husband's *ie*.

Thus the education system became a vehicle to prepare society for an overseas war of aggression. After the Sino-Japanese war the government promoted the establishment of secondary school institutions for women also, because intelligence and a national consciousness were thought strongly desirable in those who were expected to raise children. Women's education was regarded as important for other reasons too; as a means of raising the quality and standards of low-wage labour necessary for the accumulation of capital, and to prevent the spread of 'evil ideas' such as labour and women's liberation movements. By late Meiji the attendance rate for girl's compulsory education had improved, and the number of girls going on to secondary schooling had also increased. Girls were enclosed by the school system as much as boys were, but the content of their education was different. The cultivation of a 'good wife and wise mother' was the principle on which girls' education was based, so as to foster their 'essential qualities.'

While the state reinforced itself through disseminating *ie* ideology amongst the common classes where it took root, the very foundation of the commoners *ie* was being undermined. The industrial revolution and development of capitalism, concentration of land ownership with one section of landowners, loss of workers to the war and burden of heavy taxes, severely impoverished farming villages and reduced the lives of the workers and urban middle and lower classes to poverty. The efficacy of the householder's authority also, ironically, began to waver, weakened by intensified shifts in population and the emergence of couple-centered households who moved to the city away from the place where their *koseki* was registered. Further shifts occurred in the Taisho era during the First World War, when ideas of freedom and democracy flourished, criticism of the *ie* system was heightened and women's movements also developed, calling for emancipation from its fetters.

In the lead-up to the Pacific War, the government became increasingly militaristic and nationalistic, further stressing the notions of a 'family-state' and 'ancestor reverence and veneration.' "The Subjects' Path" put out by the Ministry of Education in 1941, taught that "the subects' path is to unite one hundred million hearts into one and faithfully follow the Emperor, beloved of all the people," and that "filial devotion to one's *ie* must be the same as loyalty to the Emperor. Loyalty and filial piety are not two, but one and the same thing." The requisite hierarchy within the *ie* was set out as follows; "the *ie* of our country are united by the focus on the head of the house," and "with parent-child relationships as central, the head of the house is the focus and not, as in western countries, the husband and wife." It also stated that "the household head and family, parent and child, husband and wife, brother and sister - each relationship has its place in well-regulated order; our ancestors are venerated as if present, and future family descendants are included in the notion of perpetuity of the *ie*."

5. Ancestors and the Ie after Defeat

In 1946, the year after defeat in World War II, the *ie* as a system was abolished and the Civil Code drastically revised to concur with the spirit of the new constitution, guaranteeing the freedom to marry and divorce on the basis of male and female equality. The *koseki* law was also amended so that upon marriage a woman did not legally enter the *ie* of her husband as previously, but the married couple would start a new *koseki*. Thus the legal basis for perpetuity of the *ie*, was lost. It was inevitable that general views of ancestors and ancestor worship would undergo changes.

From research into ancestor worship in urban families, Komoto Mitsugi drew the following hypotheses regarding the process of the disintegration of the *ie* as the base of traditional ancestor worship, and changes to ancestor worship in contemporary society.[7]

"A. The scale of families was reduced and became nuclear through industrialisation and urbanisation,

B. Post-war changes to the Civil Code were a turning point in the spread of couple-centred families,

C. The *ie* system based on direct lineage subsequently began to decline, and

D. Accordingly, the genealogical view of ancestor worship which held perpetuation of the *ie* as the primary duty, was changed or lost

E. Adaption of ancestor worship to a couple-based family became conspicuous; ancestors of both spouses were worshipped and limited to those within recollection."

To investigate these hypotheses, Komoto carried out a fact-finding survey on methods of worship and the maintenance of burial plots, family Buddhist altars and mortuary tablets in urban society. He also surveyed the views and practices of ancestor worship in new religions which stress ancestor worship, such as the lay religious organisation Reiyukai and its offshoots. As a result, he deduced that the family head is the heir to ancestor worship ceremonies; the normative restraint of having to be the successor is weakening; and there was strong worship of closely related ancestors for whom personal affection was held. There was, however, a punitive aspect to the latter, in the sense that it is not for divine protection, but because the hardships of present descendants are seen as divine punishment for the sufferings of ancestors.[8] Such changes in the views on ancestors and ancestor worship, correspond to the insecure lives of urban settlers and

---

[7] Komoto Mitsugi, "Ie" no Henshitsu to Senzosaishi in Kingendai ni Okeru "Ie" no Henshitsu to Shukyo, ed. Morioka Kiyomi, Shinchi Shobo, 1986.
Gendai Toshi no Minzoku Shinko - Kakyosaiken to Chinkon in Gendaijin no Shukyo, edited by Omura Eisho and Nishiyama Shigeru, Yuhikaku, Tokyo, 1988.

[8] Because burial plots are difficult to shift and new ones hard to obtain, the normative restraint of who ought to be supported has become more strongly apparent, however it has become easier to incorporate personal affection for deceased through family altars and mortuary tablets (Komoto Mitsugi, ibid.).

their weakening ability to cope with the isolation and crises, the instability of modern and contemporary society, and breakdown of families.

Members of religious sects such as Reiyukai believe that all children, not just the eldest son, should worship their ancestors, a belief which reflects the adaption of people to urban life after the industrialisation of Japanese society. Komoto believes that people who streamed into the cities to live, prayed to the ancestors of both spouses for peaceful and happy lives, because they had to survive as couples instead of in extended family groups. It was the urban dwellers without family wealth and unable to sustain family businesses, who became conscious of divine punishment and worshipped ancestors on both sides. Acceptance of this principle provided a much more satisfactory explanation for the sense of the suffering in their lives.

Komoto further states that despite the decline of the *ie* as a base, ancestor worship was preserved even while in the process of change, because the Japanese people's lives are grounded in a relativistic view of humanity. In a relativistic view as opposed to an individualistic one, relationships are understood not as an expediency, but as the basis of ones own existence, linked in a mutual existence with others. Ancestor worship, therefore, in addition to being a symbolic gesture unifying the family as a group, also "connotes a function for giving the self a foundation in society" to the members of that group. Consequently, Komoto surmises, "ancestor worship will not disappear as long as the Japanese peoples view of individualism does not change."

While I do not agree with this interpretation of individualism, the background and changes to ancestor worship and the *ie* in modern and contemporary Japanese society, can generally be viewed in this way. There is, however, one point on which I would take issue - who is the subject of this "view of ancestors?" Is only the family head or the male who will eventually become family head assumed as the subject, if not, then is it not assumed that the wife has exactly the same views on ancestors as her husband? Concluding that the significance of the *ie* is the same for women as it is for men, seems too hasty. It should not be forgotten that in principle women enter their husbands' *ie* from outside, and in contrast to men who leave the house to work, the *ie*, as the setting for the home and family life, is the only "place where women should be." The *ie* as a system regulated men's mode of existence, and thus women's mode of existence was also regulated.

It is significant that many of the new religious groups which emerged in Japan after the closing days of the shogunate, placed great emphasis on ancestor memorial rituals in the practice of their doctrine and beliefs and were essentially supported by women. Furthermore, in the view of salvation that new religious movements present, separate gender roles are frequently endowed with a sacred meaning which it is mankind's natural obligation to fulfill, and it is taught that by accomplishing this, "the sacred order" of the universe will be restored. It seems likely that the expansion of religious influence which consolidated the new religous movements, is closely connected to the birth of the housewife in Japanese society during the Taisho era, becoming subject to ambition, and popularisation of the 'housewife' in the period of rapid economic growth following the Second World War.

6. The Ambition to be a Housewife

In this paper the word housewife means a married woman economically dependent on her wage earning husband, in charge of housekeeping, housework and child rearing in the home, a place which is separate from the site of production. That is to say, the housewife was a role created for women in modern society, when the site of production, that is the workplace, was separated from the living place through industrialisation and urbanisation, and a new class of families emerged who could survive on the husband's wages alone.

The housewife engaged full-time with housework and child-rearing who saw the home as the natural place to be, emerged in Europe during the last half of the eighteenth century with the industrial revolution and development of capitalism.[9] The new bourgeois middle-class sought wealth and political power, and formed a standard of morality to underpin their particular way of life. They idealised and imitated the aristocrats, and so like the aristocracy, middle class men did not have their wives work outside the home, regarding this as evidence of economic and social success.

The role expected of the wife thus liberated from production work, was as guardian of the family against worldly intrusions, responsible for bringing up and educating children in a moral and Christian environment. Military and economic needs of the modern nation also made demands on improving the quality and environment of children's education. Fathers working outside the home could not possibly respond to these demands, therefore the mother was absolutely necessary for the chidren's upbringing before going to school. The role of mother came to be considered women's true, natural character, and the 'myth of motherhood' as the most important role for women, was formed.

By the late nineteenth century, the modern gender-based division of labour, whereby men went out to work and women took charge of housework and child rearing at home, had come to be seen as the ideal by married couples, even in the working class. This ideal was broadly realised when economic standards rose after the turn of the twentieth century, but it had already been preceded by the diffusion of the idea that the wife working outside the home was an unfortunate situation, and somehow discreditable. Throughout the nineteenth century there were very few working class families who could live on the wages of the husband alone. In spite of this, as is pointed out by Diana Gittins, "the aim of one breadwinning man per house is one of the most fundamental changes to modern family ideology; having a dramatic influence over the concepts of fatherhood, masculinity, motherhood,

---

[9] Anne Oakley, Shufu no Tanjo (Housewife, Allen Lane, 1974) transl. Okashima Chika, Sanseido, Tokyo, 1986.

femininity, family life and family policy, and continuing to influence even now."[10]

The modern housewife appeared in Japanese society during the Taisho period (1912-26), and was limited mainly to the large cities. Those who came to be called housewives were the wives of a new middle class composed of government officials, teachers, and men working in private enterprise. These women did not need to work outside the home because of the level of their husband's wages, and could concentrate full-time on housework and child-rearing. In farming families with several generations living together, the family head managed all family finances, and a wife could not preside over the housekeeping as mistress immediately after marriage if her mother-in-law did not relinquish the position. In cities, however, where families were centred on couples, any woman could become mistress of the house immediately after marriage and take responsibility for managing family matters and finances.

In Japan too, as in Europe, to make a wife work outside the home injured a man's reputation and and so being a good wife and mother, bringing up the children well and skilfully managing the husband's income came to be thought of as a woman's role and matter of pride. But even though these housewives were dependent economically on their husbands, they did not need to devote themselves solely to obeying their husband and master. It was possible for them to acquire authority in the home as husbands became dependent on their wives' exertions, and as the parent responsible for bringing up the children, a mother had much influence over them. Housewives having authority in the home does not contravene the criteria for a good wife and wise mother. On the contrary, women who skilfully exercised such authority, were able to nurse the illusion that they were being faithful to the precepts taught by women's educators that "women's duty [is] based on the natural distinctions between the sexes," and that "women are complementary to and have the same worth as men." The notion of

[10] Diana Gittins, Kazoku wo Meguru Gimon - Kotei Kannen e no Chosen (The Family in Question - Changing Household and Familiar Ideologies, Macmillan 1985) translated by Kanai Yoshiko and Ishikawa Reiko, Shinyosha, Tokyo, 1990.

the good wife and wise mother has, even today, still not lost its efficacy; it is commonly understood that "sharing the roles of work and the home according to their sex is 'natural' for men and women, and owing to these roles being complementary, they are on an equal footing."[11]

It was necessary for wives of the urban lower class to work outside as well as do the housework in order to supplement the family income. For such women, being a housewife able to live on the husbands salary alone, signified liberation from overwork and rising to a socially successful class. Consequently, 'housewife' was a desirable and longed for status for women of a class who had little hope of attaining that lifestyle even after marriage. Women who wanted to concentrate their energies on work in the same way as men, also emerged, but the idea that a woman's duty was in the home had become mainstream and a sense of discrimination toward working women was fostered.

The ambition to be a housewife was realised on a mass-scale in Japanese society from 1975 onwards during the period of rapid economic growth after World War II. With a greater inclination towards economic independence for women and a labour shortage, however, the number of wives working outside increased and the meaning of the word housewife changed. Wives who also worked outside were called *kengyo shufu*, meaning housewives with jobs, and those who were housewives in the original sense of the word, engaged full-time in housework and child-rearing, came to be known as *sengyo shufu*, or specialist housewives.

7. Ancestors as Saviours

Housewives' motivation for desiring authority was to receive society's approbation and approval, but it could also be to restore self-confidence after a break-down of family life. Feeling frustrated and having lost face as a housewife, a woman would be anxious to restore

---

[11] Koyama Shizuko, Ryosai Kembo to Iu Kihan, Keiso Shobo, 1991.

honour as a wife and wish for the strength to manage her husband and children to rebuild family life. The exercise of that authority, desired in particular by housewives who have failed in some way, was endowed with a religious authority through the memorial rituals for ancestors that new religions such as Reiyukai preach.

Reiyukai originally started from a group called Rei no Tomo (Friends of Spirits) founded by Kubo Kakutaro, a student of Tanaka Chigaku's nationalistic style of Nichiren Buddhism, Kubo's acquaintance the ascetic Wakatsuki Chise, and others. Kubo had been received as an adopted son in an *ie* of high social standing with the expectation of becoming the heir, however his adoptive mother was a woman who was difficult to please. These were his circumstances at the time he came in contact with the teachings of the *Hokke* ascetic Nishida Toshizo, through his brother Kotani Yasukichi, a believer in *Hokkekyo* (the Lotus Sutra). Nishida became a believer in the Lotus Sutra after a childhood illness; during the First World War he developed his unique belief that the true meaning of the Lotus sutra was to hold memorial services for all spirits, and so began missionary activities. He preached the equality of all people and memorial rituals for their souls, and that memorial rituals for the myriad of unworshipped spirits in order to rebuild the country were the urgent business of the whole nation.

Kubo came in contact with these teachings of Nishida, and further reached his own unique interpretation that memorial rituals for all spirits could be epitomised by memorial rituals for ancestors. This was the conviction with which he formed Rei no Tomo together with spiritualist Wakatsuki, whom he met while training at a *Hokke* branch temple. They were not able to collect enough members, but Kubo decided that he would like to form the group and engage in missionary activities. In 1924 (Taisho 13), the year after the great Kanto earthquake, his brother's second wife, Kotani Kimi, joined *Hokkekyo* to heal her husbands sickness, and Kubo took advantage of this to rigourously train and instruct her so that she became successful as a spiritualist. From 1925 he began missionary activities and in 1930 the Dai Nippon Reiyukai was established with Kimi as president and

Kubo as chairman. (Originally Baron Nagayama was president and Kimi was honorary chairman, but the Baron resigned after three months).

The name Reiyukai implies that one's own soul and the myriad of other souls are linked. Members believe that the soul is reincarnated for eternity, and so the souls of people living now could have been at some time parents, children, brothers or sisters. Worship is therefore focused on the family, including all traceable kin, with adherents giving thanks for the blessing of those spirits on the self of today, and praying for their divine protection. The sect bestowed posthumous Buddhist names, and ancestors on both the husband's and the wife's side are worshipped. By virtue of the whole family's penitence and cleansing of sins, bad karma from the past is severed, the family is saved by receiving the divine protection of ancestors spirits, and the country put at peace. This, it was taught, is the duty of the people.

Nishida's spiritual outlook implied equality of all people. In Reiyukai, however, all phenomenon of this world were linked to the spirits of ancestors and the *ie*, the causes and effect of fate were stressed, and sickness and suffering in the present world were regarded as the result of actions in the past.[12] At the time this interpretation was formulated, there was no questioning of the structural contradictions in society, and circumstances were regarded more as a question of someone's attitude, therefore solutions were sought through confession and penitence. The beliefs of Reiyukai, which base ancestor memorial rituals on this kind of spiritual view and concept of salvation, reinforce the *ie* family ethic, moral standards and concept of the nation as a family. During the Pacific War when many new religious groups were suppressed under strengthened government ideological control, Reiyukai was an exception and actually managed to extend its influence. Kubo died in 1944, but Kimi, taking her cue from "assisting the imperial rule" activities of the Patriotic Women's Association,

---

[12] Kubo Kakutaro felt a deep sense of responsibility at entering the Kubo family as successor to the *katoku*. Though a man, his position was similar to that of a bride, and this is possibly the reason why he regarded ancestor memorial services as so important.

organised a women's group and encouraged women to be ready to do the utmost for their country in protecting the home front.[13]

Helen Hardacre discovered from her research into Reiyukai in the latter 1970s, that the members' greatest aim and interest was rebuilding the home and family, and many desired the return of the *ie* ethic.[14] Not only Reiyukai and its offshoots, but many new religions endow marriage and family with a religious meaning, attaching importance to the woman's role in the family and furthermore identifying this with the proper worship of ancestors. In some respects new religions can be seen as popular self-help movements, because the kind of salvation they offer is attainable in this world. This salvation is not that of the next life or world that traditional Buddhism teaches, but one which promises deliverance from the suffering of poverty, sickness and war during this life. Such a concept of salvation stems from a world view which regards people and their lives as the place where the great soul of the sacred cosmos ought to be manifest.

At this point, individual desire for salvation in this world is merged with greater ambition of salvation for all people, to become the salvation of all human beings' existence. Home and family are not beyond reach of sacred power, they are the very places overflowing with holiness, where the highest values can be realised, and the prosperity of the country and order in the world can be achieved through attaining the proper order.

8. Ancestors as a Channel for Power

New religious groups teach that to overcome some crisis or anguish one should not try to change the people around you such as husband, children or mother-in-law, rather one should reflect on one's own selfishness and self-centered ego, and try to change one's own

---

[13] Murakami Shigeyoshi, Nippon Hyakunen no Shukyo - Haibutsukishyaku kara Sokagakkai made, Kodansha, Tokyo, 1968.

[14] Helen Hardacre, "Lay Buddhism in Contemporary Japan Reiyukai Kyodan," Princeton University Press, Princeton, 1984.

disposition. This attitude is expressed in the word *sagaru*, meaning to step back and defer to others. Women in particular are meant to 'defer to their husbands' and 'give their husband his proper place.' Senior sect members would counsel younger women that if, for example, their husbands became violently drunk or had affairs, it is "because you have not performed your duties as a wife adequately," and you should reflect on this and confess to your husband.

Hardacre calls this kind of problem solving "the strategy of the weak." This strategy is used by those in a socially weak position when they try to create an advantageous situation for themself. Wives who internalise the moral standard that they should defer to their husbands, must find the means to manipulate their husbands in order to realise their own objects. The so-called attitude of *sagaru*, is actually a fairly effective method for the supposedly subordinate wife to secure the power to achieve the happiness she desires for her family. This strategy can operate successfully in Japanese society, because it is not uncommon for a husband who may be secretly feeling guilty about his shortcomings in fulfilling his duties as a husband, to appreciate his wife's taking this attitude.[15]

Komoto Mitsugi, mentioned earlier, writes that in new religious groups descended from Reiyukai the ancestors of both spouses are worshipped by all the children and not just the heir. He sees this as a reflection of the instability of urban families, but then it seems that Komoto does not regard the urban family lifestyle as a desirable one. Men aside, for women the urban household was one which, if unstable, could be built by a couple themselves and was a place where positive values could be discovered. Ancestors and the *ie* would have a somewhat different significance for housewives in this position.

Despite having left their hometowns, the *ie* was an integral part of state authority and this together with ancestor worship and the *ie* as a means of delineating self-identity, made it still a powerful source of

---

[15] This strategy is based on the assumption that the one who takes the initiative in recognising their sins first is in a position of moral superiority, and is common behaviour in Japan. Men also engage in the strategy of *sagaru*, which is not something unique devised by new religions for the benefit of women only.

meaning for urban dwellers. It is conceivable that worshipping ancestors of the *ie* held an important meaning for urban men, but on the other hand, it seems that urban male salaried workers increasingly found their sense of identity and belonging through their work, in public office or private industry. Housewives, however, as long as they complied with the norms for the sexual division of roles and labour, did not have any means of giving the self social significance through identification with a group, apart from as the housewife of a certain *ie*.

Marriage in the *ie* system was not a means of fulfilling a couple's desire to be together, but was intended for the sake of perpetuating the *ie* itself. Women therefore had to submit to the authority of the head of the family, usually their husband, who would be criticised if the conventions of *ie* ideology were openly flouted and he allowed himself to be ruled by his wife. Yet it was not such conflict with the *ie* ideology that housewives dreamt of, but to be a good wife ensuring matrimonial harmony as the imperial rescript on education urged, and if she could respond to the expectations of the nation by becoming a good mother her own position in the home would be strengthened and she would be highly regarded by society.

When the family unit is in a state of crisis, according to the criterion for the sexual division of roles and work, it is the housewife whose mission it is to heal the members woes. Wives who were followers of a new religion and tried to heal their families according to its teachings, which placed the teaching and practice of memorial rituals for ancestors at their core, secured a religious meaning and sanctification of their mission through ancestor worship, with the authority of ancestors in the background. In the world of the *ie*, participation in memorial rituals for ancestors was, as was bearing and bringing up a successor to the *ie*, an essential route for a woman to integrate herself as a proper member of her husband's family. The authority of the head of the house, as successor to the memorial ritual for ancestors, bore the burden of legitimising this authority. In families where the legitimisation of authority was shared to a certain degree, the wife could place herself in a position of power and authority over all the family, by taking care of the ancestor rituals as her husband's executor, and positioning herself as the subject of the ancestral rituals and the one who realised the will of the ancestors in the house.

New religious movements born after the shogunate, were also ideological and activist movements of the common people for independence from professional religious leaders grown attached to power. They attempted to endow themselves with religious authority by establishing rituals which held religious significance. The memorial rituals for ancestors which socially frustrated people staked their salvation on, were a means of conforming to the *ie* value system permeating Japanese society. This independent rereading of official *ie* ideology by the masses was simultaneously a pursuit of power to control the spirit, or soul, symbolised by the "ancestors of the house," and an attempt to take back into their hands the authority to regulate their own fate. Because housewives were the chief supporters of new religons, women who accepted the teaching of new religions that a woman's duty was to keep the sacred order in the home and abide by the principles of *tateru* (honour) and *sagaru* (defer), endowed themselves with a religious authority by the conscientous practise of these teachings and gave a meaning for existence of the self. Thus women became subjects of the 'truth system' to which they subordinated themselves and which sanctified a criteria for the divison of roles and labour by gender.[16]

A 'truth system' is a set of ideas by which a certain social group comprehends the world; it enables possible meaning and understanding, to think about and work in the world, and sets the effective limits for the basis of meaning for members of a society. People enveloped in a certain 'truth system', regard as obvious and justify the events of daily life that occur according to this body of truths, and by doing so suspend consideration and judgement. When the basis of consideration and judgement is questioned closely and the answer is "it's natural" or "of course anyone would think that," that person is coming up against the boundaries of the system of truth on

---

[16] Igeta Midori, 'Shufu no Matsuru' Senzo - Juzokusuru Shutai in Gendai Shukyo Gaku 4 Ken-i no Kochiku to Hakai edited by Wakimoto Tsuneya and Yanagawa Keiichi, Tokyo University Press, Tokyo, 1992

which they depend. The truth system enveloping the whole of society is a complex one derived from more than one system. A person acknowledged as having a thorough knowledge of a certain truth system is able to exercise authority over others in accordance with the degree to which that system is held in regard by society.

At the very least, since pre-modern times in Japanese society, ancestor worship was both the most familiar and highly valued system of truth employed in defending the community. The teachings of new religious groups which place high regard on memorial rituals for ancestors, opened up a channel to power for women through ancestor worship. Women became the subject of ancestor worship, those who carry out the ancestors' will, and as such gained authority within the bounds that family and society recognise the authority of ancestors. In new religious groups like Reiyukai, if a wife integrates her own ancestors as the ancestors of her husband's *ie*, she is able to strongly impress on the family that perpetuation of the *ie* actually depends on cooperative relations with her husband.

Such views on ancestor worship were very quickly adapted during the rapid urbanization and industrialization of Japanese society after defeat in World War II. But even while new ideas like equal rights for men and women, and couple centered families were being absorbed, *ie* ideology concomitant with the illusion of 'a homogeneous people' descended from the Emperor's ancestors, remained as ever. The object of those who inherited *ie* ideology was a rich family life based on the premise of the gender based division of labour that industry demanded. The result of relinquishing an army was that men became independent of such yearnings, and were incorporated instead into a hierarchical structure of authority which pivoted on industry and integrated a value system of giving priority only to economical returns.

9. A Channel for Power

New religions recommend members that "in order for teachings to be truly understood," they should visit the facilities regularly, participate in assemblies, and receive counselling directly from senior members. They also teach that one's own salvation depends on praying for the salvation of others, introducing new members, and passing on the teachings. If salvation depends on saving as many people as possible, then simply staying at home will not help achieve that end, and so women who firmly believed that their natural place was in the home, diligently went out on religious activities in order to defend it. If she succeeded in finding salvation for herself and many others as well, and this were recognised by other believers, then a woman could rise up through the group hierarchy and secure authority and power to direct other group members. A rise in status within the group, as Helen Hardacre has also pointed out, also meant the possibility of increasing her authority at home. It could reasonably be concluded that these factors motivate women believers to enthusiastically participate in religious activities. Housewives discovered a way of linking their own desires and energies to the world outside the house, while keeping intact a sense of themselves and their position in the home.

Women's experiences in the war also played a part in their desire to leave the house afterwards. During the war they were very keen to participate in public activities, and were reluctant to give up everything even after the men had returned home. Through the system of national mobilisation, women had advanced into the men's workplace and also had been made to participate in activities like the National Defense Women's Association. Although compulsory, participating in public activities outside the home, was a contribution to society which gave women a sense of satisfaction, confidence in their own abilities, and a sense of liberation at going outside of the *ie* even for just a brief space of time. Such experiences were the foundations for nationwide women's group activities after the war.[17]

When women desire authority and wish to enter the hierarchy of power and authority occupied by men, they can forge their own way or use the system itself to open up a channel. There is also the option of

[17] Tani Mikiko, Senso wo Ikita Onnatachi - Shogen Kokubo Fujinkai, Minerva Shobo, Kyoto, 1985; Horiba Kiyoko, Inaguyananabachi - Okinawa Joseishi wo Saguru, Domesu Shuppan, Tokyo, 1990.

rejecting the hierarchical structure of authority itself. Yet the direction chosen by women disillusioned with the housewife's role, was none of these. Accepting the existing power structures, they sought authority by fulfilling women's allotted role. The teachings of new religions which stress "an altruistic heart," "becoming a person of use to others", "praying for other people's and other families' happiness, and cooperating," can divert women's energy and hopes for the "happiness of the family" from their own *ie* towards the religious sect and hence to the world outside the sect. This probably saves their energy from being entirely subsumed by the family, nevertheless the fact remains that the absolute gender-based division of roles and labour is reinforced, bolstering a social order in which such division of roles is essential. Women's energies were drawn into the power structure of the industrialised state.

Women who introduced the beliefs of new religions into the *ie* have been criticised because the method of worshipping ancestors is not traditional, yet they maintain that they are practising correct ancestor memorial rituals. Society tends to cast doubtful eyes at new religious groups, and it is easy to think of these women also as engrossed in something questionable. Nevertheless, if it is understood that they are attempting to restore the sacred value of the *ie*, the risk of being criticised and censured by people around them is reduced. The whole of Japanese society is enveloped in a truth system which does not doubt the sacredness of the *ie*, home, and family blood-ties, and to doubt or to deny this is to touch on the strongest taboo in society.

The truth system safeguarded by an inviolable taboo, suppresses doubts about the man-made social order, the structure of power and its very existence, and forces our thoughts into submission. The absolute viewpoint of the truth system which prescribes relations between people, is also a symbolic logic system which differentiates them, creating groups to be discriminated against and excluded by society as fearful and defiled.[18] To become conscious of the limits of our own

---

[18] As Yamasaki Kaoru points out in Ishahyosho no Kozo, in *Sabetsu Mondai Kenkyu* 1 - Sabetsu no Teigi wo Meggute Sabetsu Mondai wo Kangaerukai,

perception of the world, and the logic behind discrimination and exclusion in Japanese society, then we must go beyond the illusion of the state, comprising the *ie*, home, family blood-ties, being the equivalent of a truth system.

To simply reject the illusions fostered by the state is not enough, there must be a constant awareness and continual effort. We have not tried to subjugate the artificial systems of the *ie*, the state which fundamentally prescribes modern and contemporary society, and a truth system which does not tolerate doubts about the existence of these. A channel for power, for both men and women, is linked to the existing order and structure of authority, and the energy poured into the pursuit of such ambitions, only serves to bolster a state which maintains its identity through discrimination and exclusion.

(Akashi Shoten, Tokyo, 1992), when human relations or social ties are a problem, the coupling of 'self' and 'other' are always in the debate. "In order for [this] structural relation of self-other, I-you, to come into being, there must first be people excluded on the outer who are the aliens and outsiders."

Women and Soka Gakkai

Haga Akira

1. A Shaky Soka Gakkai

No religious organisation in the world of Japanese religions draws the attention of the mass media as constantly as Soka Gakkai. Of all the numerous lay religious groups, not only does the Soka Gakkai claim to be the largest with the most believers, but it is also the only religious organisation to have spawned a political party. As the second largest opposition party, Komeito, or the Clean Government Party, are in the powerful position of holding the casting vote in politics, for which reason Soka Gakkai is highly influential both socially and politically.

In the past, the organisation's image has been marred by a number of scandals inappropriate for a religious group, ranging from Electoral Law violations; to obstruction of freedom of speech through the attempted prevention of the publication of a book critical of the organisation; phone-tapping; unauthorised duplication of the main religious image of Nichiren Shoshu (the parent sect); rebellion within the ranks of the Central Executive Committee; internal accusations; sex scandals involving long-term Gakkai President Ikeda Daisaku; official corruption involving Komeito Diet members, and so on. However, the recent dispute with the parent sect Nichiren Shoshu, is an issue which touches the very core of the faith, and as such has elicited greater unease and anguish amongst followers than ever before.

Diligence in devotional activities as a Soka Gakkai member does not stop with the pursuit of the happiness of the individual; rather, the religion teaches that true happiness lies in pursuing the greater ideal of *kosen rufu*, the conversion of the entire world. It is the drive of members who believe in this and pride themselves on their earnest approach to Gakkai activities, who find therein their raison d'etre and have been responsible for disseminating the teachings and supporting the organisation. Many members, however, have become suspicious of the frequent scandals and discrepancies between ideals and the reality, and weary of the burdensome schedule of activities and heavy financial load, have elected to leave the sect.

Excommunication by the parent sect generally elicited one of four reactions from Soka Gakkai members. Many older long-term members, unable to contemplate carrying out their devotions without access to the Nichiren temple, elected to leave the Soka Gakkai and join the parent sect. Others who had been strongly associated with the Gakkai felt that departure from the organisation would mean denial of their own existence, and so cast their lot in with other remaining members and put their trust in Ikeda. They closed their eyes and ears to outside criticism and resolved to stay with Soka Gakkai to the last. A third group, disillusioned with both the Gakkai and the Nichiren sect, chose to abandon both, while a fourth group, although shaken with doubts and suspicions, were frightened by stories of harassment and reprisals others had been subjected to, and so resigned themselves to remaining as members, fearing punishment if they decided to leave.

2. My Own Experience with the Soka Gakkai

My first contact with Soka Gakkai was in 1957, when Toda Josei was president. The woman I was boarding with in Shibuya, Tokyo was a devoted Soka Gakkai member, and I happened to fall ill whilst living there with a relapse of pulmonary tuberculosis. Suddenly I was a target for conversion.

The first time I fell ill with TB was during my final year when preparing for exams at a girls' school in Kyushu during World War Two. I entered a long period of convalescence and had to abandon the idea of continuing with my education, a major setback for me as I started out on my young adult life. Some years later, not having forsaken original ambitions, I came to Tokyo to continue my education, only to suffer a repeat attack and returned home to Kyushu. I reverted to a life of convalescence and my marriageable age passed me by.

Eventually I returned to Tokyo, only to suffer another attack, and at this point I lost all confidence and began to despair.

The succession of ill-fortune which made my youth a period of anxiety contributed to the circumstances which gave me sufficient reason to join a religion. I was moved by the words used to convert me, that if I were to believe in the main image and chant the Nichiren prayer, my life force would be strengthened, I would be made well, and my bad fate could be reversed. In any event, I had to conquer this illness. Soka Gakkai's image at that time however, with its dogmatic attacks on other religions and forced conversion practices, was that of a radical group with a dubious reputation, and I had reservations about becoming a member of such an organisation. It was during this time of uncertainty that my landlady gave me some Gakkai publications and teaching texts with the recommendation to read them.

I had only a vague general knowledge of Buddhism, and learnt a great deal from those materials:

"The Buddhist teaching of the great teacher Nichiren is a philosophy that explains the true nature of the universe, of life itself. It is not just a philosophy, but involves a practice which aims to transform your life, to perfect your character. Furthermore, it goes beyond the level of the individual, to hold as its goal the achievement of peace and prosperity for the whole of mankind."

"Now that Western civilisation, based as it is on Christian thought, has reached a stalemate, Buddhist law, said to be the wisdom of the East, has the potential to lead world thought."

"Soka Gakkai is a group practising for total revolution which takes as its basic doctrine the spirit of Buddhist law."

Won over by clearly defined argument and a grand concept, I decided to join. With the initial determination to save myself from my sickness, I chanted the Nichiren prayer with zeal and attended the meetings.

I was encouraged by one paragraph in Nichiren's writings which reads "Namu Myoho Renge Kyo is like the roar of a lion. What sickness can therefore be an obstacle?"[1] Little by little I began to feel the life force begin to flow through my veins and I started on the road back to good health, becoming a firm believer in the good karma of the newly converted.

At the time, the Gakkai was drastically increasing its membership through aggressive conversion activities known as the Great Shakubuku Drive. Day and night, members were told that proselytising itself was a practice of Buddhist teaching, and that people who did so were messengers of Buddha, so that the conversion of others meant an accumulation of virtue, in dimensions immeasurable by the human intellect. But I was inept at conversion; I was far too embarrassed to speak to people with some assumed air of knowledge to convince them to join, when my own learning was so superficial and my own faith still unconfirmed. In response I was told that carrying out the work of Buddha through speech would act to strengthen my faith as I spoke to people, and that the Buddhist teaching was the religion capable of unconditionally saving all people. Keeping it to myself and not telling others about it would amount to disparagement of Buddha's teachings. In this way, I was gradually cornered. I was told that if unable to proselytise by myself, at least I could cooperate by accompanying others who were. When I had a date on a day off I was pressured with the question of which activity was of higher value, dating or devotional activities, and in this way was forced to go out. I began to resent this coercive approach, and became distressed by the threatening interference and control of my private life. I did not want to be bound by this organisation - I wanted to be spiritually free.

Eventually I married a man who was critical of and averse to Soka Gakkai, so I was able to escape the organisation by using the opposition of my husband as an excuse to resist attempts at reconversion. Some years later a Soka Gakkai council executive moved in next door, and association with his family provided me with the opportunity of attending my first Gakkai meeting in a long time. I

---

[1] Reply to Kyo'o.

had not been blessed with children and felt that something was lacking in my life, so was looking for something to provide me with emotional and spiritual support. I wanted to study the teachings more seriously, but by this time Soka Gakkai had swelled to become a gigantic organisation, Ikeda was being idolised, the "Soka teachings" were being propagated, and friction with the parent sect Nichiren Shoshu had begun. When I learned that a doctrinal severing from Nichiren was indicated, I was totally confused. Shortly after, the series of scandals just mentioned began to occur in succession, leaving me in shock. I could not possibly remain faithful to such a religious group, and so once again withdrew from the organisation.

But I did not discard my faith. The image that I had prayed to so earnestly at the time I joined Soka Gakkai remains enshrined in my room, and although I could not be called persistent or devoted, I remain a believer of the Lotus Sutra in my own way. Buddhist law remains the basis of my view of the world and humanity, but I intend to continue to study religions in general for the rest of my life, without adhering to any particular religion or sect.

Although no longer a part of the organisation, I am always conscious of Soka Gakkai, and carefully collect every possible piece of information related to it. This feeling of ambivalence, whereby despite my criticism I still feel attached, is a due to the respect I have in some ways for the ideals and practices of the Soka Gakkai, and a kind of nostalgia I have as a past member.

The theme of this paper is "feminism and religion." When religion is considered from a feminist viewpoint, there is no avoiding the assumption of a critical standpoint concerning the deep-rooted ideas of discrimination against women which exist in religion, and also in Buddhism.

I share deep feelings of empathy with the experiences and perplexities of the women members of Soka Gakkai whom I have written about here.

3. The Lotus Sutra and Female Attainment of Buddhahood

The single-handed control of Soka Gakkai by Ikeda Daisaku, is recognised both within and without the organisation. Of the members who support this patriarchal structure, it is the obedient and faithful women's section which is particularly powerful.

The reason there are so many female believers in sects of the Nichiren lineage, which take the Lotus Sutra as the basis of their teachings, is that this sutra was the first to teach of women attaining buddhahood. Nichiren esteemed the Lotus Sutra in particular as the supreme sutra, and actively taught that women could attain the state of buddhahood.

In Chapter 12 of the Devadatta, the Lotus Sutra speaks of female attainment of enlightenment. Sariputra, lauded as the wisest of the Buddha's disciples, puts a question to an eight-year-old daughter of the dragon king.

"You say that you will soon attain the highest path. This is difficult to believe. Why is this? The female body is polluted; it is not a fit vessel for the Dharma. How can you attain the highest enlightenment? The Buddha path is long. One can only attain it after diligently carrying out severe practices, and completely practicing the perfections over immeasurable *kalpas*. Moreover, the female body has five obstructions. How can you with your female body quickly become a Buddha?"

Then the daughter of the dragon king presented to Buddha a jewel worth the great manifold cosmos, Buddha accepted it, and in that instant she was transformed into a Buddha. "Then the assembly there all saw the daughter of the dragon king instantly transform into a man, perfect the bodhisattva practices, go to the Vimala world in the south, sit on a jewelled lotus flower and attain highest complete enlightenment, become endowed with the thirty-two marks and eighty excellent characteristics, and expound the true Dharma universally for the sake of all sentient beings in the ten directions."

On the fifth day of March, when Murasaki Shikibu (author of The Genji Monogatari) visited the palace of Emperor Tsuchimikado to hear the thirty lectures being expounded there on the Lotus Sutra, she heard the lecture on the Chapter on Devadatta from the fifth fascicle of the Sutra of the Lotus of the Wonderful Dharma, that women could also without doubt achieve the state of buddhahood, upon which she was so impressed that she recited, "On this wondrous day, the fifth day of the fifth month I have heard Buddha's teaching of the fifth fascicle."

The Lotus Sutra was a true blessing for women of that period, subjected to scorn and discrimination as they were, and told that they were in no way capable of attaining enlightenment. For women of today, however, the concept of "transforming a woman into a man," in other words the argument that a woman is incapable of attaining buddhahood without first transforming into the body of a man, is unacceptable. The concept of females transmuting to male form is well known from the following Pure Land hymn of praise written by Shinran.[2]

"By trusting in the great compassion of Amida Buddha, the miracle of Buddha wisdom will appear, and by praying for transformation from female body to male, women can also attain the state of buddhahood." This concept can also be seen in a number of other sutras such as The Sutra on the Supreme Light of Samadhi.[3] The inherence of buddha-nature in every living being[4] is held as the central concept in Mahayana Buddhism, and presumably there is no distinction between male and female in the concept of "all sentient beings."

In addition, the thirty-two major and eighty minor physical marks of a fully enlightened buddha include aspects which clearly go beyond divisions of sex, such as the concealment of the genitals within the body, extremely supple arms and legs, and lips as red as the fruit of the bimba tree. Rather than suggesting a sexless being, neither male nor female, this suggests a form encompassing both masculinity and femininity. It is indeed obvious upon viewing a Buddha image

---

[2] Buddhist priest, 1173-1262 and founder of the Pure Land sect.
[3] Unofficial translation of Bussetsu Chonichi Myozanmai Kyo.
[4] The Sutra on the Great Extinction, or Mahaparinirvana Sutra, 36th fascicle.

complete with the thirty-two major and eighty minor marks that it is endowed with both masculine and feminine characteristics.

The ultimate essence of Buddhist law is the attainment of enlightenment and becoming a Buddha, an existence which should go beyond divisions of sex to include both male and female, despite which the theory of "transformation of woman into man" appears frequently in the sutras. This demonstrates how deeply the idea of male predominance over female is rooted in Buddhism, and that the Buddhist teachings themselves are filled with contradictions.

4. Was Nichiren a Feminist?

At the beginning of the Kamakura Period, the warrior class grew powerful and the ancient society ruled by the nobility and centering around the Emperor collapsed. New reform movements flourished, even in the world of religion. Honen, Shinran and Ippen were propagating the practice of *nenbutsu* (recitation of the name of Amida Buddha), Eisai and Dogen were promoting zen, and Nichiren was preaching of salvation through the Lotus Sutra. These six sect founders of Kamakura Buddhism made Buddhist teachings, which until then had belonged only to select social classes, available to the common people, and salvation and enlightenment for women was preached. Nichiren went even one step further than the others by developing a teaching on liberation for women, attracting a large number of enthusiastic women followers.

Nichiren left behind him many essays and letters to his disciples, compiled in a single volume that is the sacred text of Soka Gakkai, "The Complete Writings of Nichiren Daiseinin." Nichiren's writings frequently allude to the attainment of buddhahood by women. In "Women's Attainment of Buddhahood," he writes that women are profoundly disliked in prior sutras, where they are described as emissaries from hell, and the sinful bearers of the five hindrances and three obediences (to father, husband, and then children), whereas the Lotus Sutra teaches of the attainment of buddhahood by the daughter of the dragon king with her present form. Nichiren teaches that "women especially should believe in this sutra."

He also touches on the attainment of enlightenment by the daughter of the dragon king in The Daimoku of the Lotus Sutra saying that "A woman who has faith in the Lotus Sutra will proceed directly to the Pure Land in the west. Such is the virtue inherent in the single character myo (one of the syllables of the Lotus Sutra daimoku). Myo means to revive, that is, to return to life."

The Opening of the Eyes is said to be one of the five major texts. It is stated within this text that "when [the dragon kings's daughter] attained Buddhahood, this does not mean simply that one person did so. It reveals the fact that all women will attain Buddhahood. In the various Hinayana sutras that were preached before the Lotus Sutra, it is denied that women can ever attain Buddhahood. In the Mahayana sutras other than the Lotus Sutra, it would appear that women can attain Buddhahood or be reborn in the pure land. But they may do so only after they have changed into some other form. It is not the kind of immediate attainment of Buddhahood that is based on the doctrine of the three thousand realms in a single moment of life. Thus it is an attainment of Buddhahood or rebirth in the pure land in name but not in reality. The dragon king's daughter represents "one example that stands for all the rest." When the dragon king's daughter attained Buddhahood, it opened up the way to attaining Buddhahood for all women of later ages."

When Nichiren teaches of women attaining Buddhahood, he makes no mention of transmutation into male form. He says that the enlightenment of the dragon king's daughter is a case of "attaining Buddhahood in one's present form", and the preceding paragraphs should be interpreted rather as a denial of any transformation from female to male.

In the Recitation of the Hoben and Juryo Chapters, (also sometimes called the Gosho on Menstruation), a female devotee, thinking a menstruating woman to be defiled, asks whether it is permissible to pray to the Buddha or to recite sutras at such times. In response, Nichiren says that menstruation does not represent any kind of pollution coming from an external source, but is rather simply a phenomenon related to the perpetuation of the seed of life and death. It is simply a female idiosyncrasy, something excreted from the human body in the same way as faeces, and so long as one observes clean habits, there are no special prohibitions to be observed related to menstruation. This serious and liberal response about the female menstrual cycle coming from Nichiren, a man who never married, is even pleasantly amusing.

Judging from this example alone, Nichiren appears to have been quite a progressive feminist for his time, making it easy to understand why he managed to draw large numbers of female followers. However, other passages in his writing give cause for scepticism. For example, the phrases most lauded by the Soka Gakkai on the way in which a woman should conduct her life, are as follows: "It is the power of the bow that determines the flight of the arrow, the might of the dragon that controls the movement of the clouds, and the strength of the wife that guides the actions of her husband" (The Bow and Arrow), and "Women support others and thereby cause others to support them." (Letter to the brothers). If this line of thought stopped here it would be acceptable, but any woman of today would be taken aback upon reading the lines that follow. "When a husband is happy, his wife will be fulfilled. If a husband is a thief, his wife will become one, too."

The next lines then made me gasp in surprise, unable to believe my eyes.

"The Chinese character for woman implies "to depend". The wisteria depends on the pine tree, and a woman depends on a man." (The Unity of Husband and Wife)
"A woman's soul is her husband. Without him, she has no soul." (The Supremacy of the Law)
"A woman is like water, which takes the shape of its container. A woman is like an arrow, which is fitted to the bow. A woman is like a ship, which is guided by its rudder. Therefore, a woman will become a thief if her husband is a thief, and she will become a queen if her husband is a king. If he is a man of virtue (who has faith in the True Law), she will become a Buddha. Not only in this

life but also in the life to come, her lot will be determined by her
husband (The Offering of a Summer Robe)."
This time I was left speechless. A woman is like a doll or a piece of
wood, totally without personality, with no subjective existence of her
own which excludes a man. A woman's life, her happiness, her
unhappiness, everything is reliant upon a man, right through into the
afterlife. Indeed!

Nichiren's writing style is ornate, sonorous, and scattered liberally
with modifiers and similes. However his concepts are based on a view
of women which cannot be dismissed as just a flourish of rhetoric. In
fact, these phrases, rather than being religious teachings, are taken
from letters which include thanks for religious services for the repose
of the dead, and therefore can be considered to reflect the view of
women as dictated by the social mores of the time. Speaking
specifically of religious instruction in these same letters, he denies the
difference between the sexes, saying "A woman who embraces the
Lotus Sutra not only exceeds all other women, but also surpasses all
men," negating differentiation on the basis of sex, and emphatically
asserting the independent existence of women with "No matter whom
you may marry, you must not follow him if he is an enemy of the
Lotus Sutra. Strengthen your faith more than ever."

The problem is that these posthumous writings of Nichiren are
employed as scriptures instead of literary works. In the Soka Gakkai,
Nichiren is defined as the true Buddha of "the period of the last and
decadent Dharma," and his writings as the teachings for this age.
Therefore his writings are sacred to believers, with every word and
phrase taught as dicta.

Read as works of literature, the reader has the pleasure of freely
forming his own opinions, evaluating his writings as great in some
parts, interesting in others, or perhaps somewhat questionable in
others, thus gaining a sense of the human aspect and the mood of the
man Nichiren. However when those same works are treated as gospel,
read by followers with profound reverence and awe, they cannot be
freely interpreted or criticised. Herein lie the pitfalls and dangers of
religion.

5. *Taking the Texts to Heart*

Soka Gakkai emphasises a teaching which is based on the writings of Nichiren. One section of his writings says "Exert yourself in the two ways of practice and study. Without practice and study, there can be no Buddhism. You must not only persevere yourself; you must also teach others. Both practice and study arise from faith. Teach others to the best of your ability, even if only a single sentence or phrase " (The True Entity of Life). Based on this writing, followers are repeatedly told that Nichiren's writings are teachings for eternity, that study of the teachings is the backbone of everything, that their hearts must be imbued with every word and every phrase of these golden teachings. The texts are studied at meetings and examinations are given, in a system where those who pass are promoted up a hierarchy of assistant teacher, teacher, assistant professor, professor and master.

The teaching that women should accord men due respect and be obedient to them, and furthermore that a man's failure to display his full potential is also his wife's responsibility, is truly tailored to man's advantage, and is useful in creating an atmosphere whereby the father rules the home. Even if discrimination against women does exist within Soka Gakkai, it is not considered to be the responsibility of the organisation.

Ikeda Daisaku has ingeniously rearranged the teachings of Nichiren to suit this day and age, and make them attractive. He deftly captures the hearts of women members by praising women as being the earth and the sun, saying that the Gakkai women's division pioneers women's liberation, and expounding that women are total human beings who can accomplish anything. In this way he inspires women to work to improve themselves, and preaches that Gakkai activities are the ideal arena in which to undergo such training. Female Gakkai members are divided into the female division of the youth section if they are unmarried, and the women's division if they are married.

Inculcated by these skilful instructions of the president on a daily basis, and taking the texts to heart, gradually the women become brainwashed, and fall under his spell. There is never word uttered about feminism or discrimination against women and an impregnable atmosphere was created that made it impossible to say anything tinged with doubt or criticism. It is more comfortable within the organisation to meekly believe and participate in activities, so the women strive for maximum performance in their daily Gakkai activities, always urging each other on to satisfy Ikeda and make him happy.

6. Women for Whom the Policy of "Obey and Be Obeyed" Went Amiss

S was twenty-eight years old when she became a Soka Gakkai member in 1955. Her husband's business had failed, incurring enormous debts, and their creditors were pressuring them daily. As well as their difficulties in meeting their basic living expenses, S was also prone to sickness, unable to stay out of hospitals for long. In addition, her relationship with the strong-willed mother-in-law she lived with, was bad. She had thus simultaneously assembled the major three motivations for joining a religion, poverty, sickness, and conflict - to result in the worst possible situation.

One day, one of her mother-in-law's friends who had come to visit strongly urged her to join Soka Gakkai, inviting her to a discussion meeting. At the time the Gakkai was developing and flourishing under its second president Toda Josei, so that the discussion meeting that S attended with O, her mother-in-law, was lively and animated. When members began to relate their own experiences, they spoke in succession of resolving problems of difficult daily lives, sickness and family disharmony through devoted accumulation of religious merits, and their experiences reversing their fortunes. One line of the study materials for that day from Nichiren's Winter Always Turns to Spring went straight to S's heart: "Those who believe in the Lotus Sutra are as if in winter, which never fails to turn into spring."

When it was time to go home, O and S had both already decided to join. The response of S's husband's was "If everything could be solved just by chanting the Nichiren prayer, there wouldn't be any suffering in the world. I'm not doing it," but he refrained from directly opposing his mother and wife's decision to join. Secretly he also hoped that the practice would work.

And so S and O's devotional life began. As the two of them chanted together morning and evening holding in their hearts the same prayer, the discordant hard feelings which had existed between them for many years seemed to gradually dissolve. For S, the stress arising out of conflict with her mother-in-law was one of the causes of her poor health, so it was the best thing that could have happened. She became brighter and healthier, and began to sell cosmetics in her spare time, so that she was able to assist with the family budget. O also helped with the housework and looking after the two children. The husband met with favourable conditions and was able to gain employment again.

O was delighted at the good fortune of a new believer, and before long related her own experiences at a discussion meeting. "I pray now that in addition to this good fortune, your son will join the faith as soon as possible." The head of the women's division, who had come to give instruction that day, looked over at S as she said this. "Whether or not a husband joins depends on the faith of his wife. If a wife, through her faith, manages to change her personality to become a good wife, there is no reason why her husband will not also be moved to act. It is written in the texts that a woman has the capacity of getting people to follow her will by first following the will of others."

S nodded nervously in agreement in front of the large number of people present. She had been educated during the war at a girls school in the Japanese tradition of "good wife, wise mother," and had never felt much resistance to the idea that a wife should respect and obey her husband. Until now she had attended to her husband in this way and put on a bright face around him, exerting herself in a manner that was almost pathetic. When her husband eventually joined, and the three of them attended a discussion meeting together, S was given a grand round of applause. Her husband also began participating in Gakkai activities, and S's work began to generate more income than she had imagined, their life went smoothly, taking a turn for the better.

In 1960, Ikeda Daisaku took office as the third Soka Gakkai president. The appearance of this young thirty-two year old awe-inspiring leader served to fuel further the organisation's burgeoning growth. The new president was immensely popular with female members.

The concepts of *kosen rufu* and *obutsu myogo* were mentioned frequently in the instruction and study sessions at every meeting and in all Soka Gakkai publications. *Kosen rufu* referred to broad propagation of Buddhist law, in other words proselytising to increase the number of believers. To seek and be satisfied only with the salvation of oneself was considered selfish. Buddhistic altruism meant teaching the Buddhist law to other people to save them, action considered to be practice of the true Buddhist path. *Obutsu myogo* referred to a concept of the fusion of government and Buddhism, in other words the implementation of politics based on the spirit of Buddhist law. People do not exist in isolation, and therefore if politics are not conducted correctly and society is not prosperous and peaceful, then the happiness of the individual cannot be attained. Soka Gakkai entered into politics as the practice of the ideal of *obutsu myogo*, and Komeito, or the Clean Government Party, came into being.

Devotion is the unified practice of the three elements of faith, action and study. Simply chanting the Nichiren prayer and reading the scriptures at home is not enough. It is the actual practice of converting people and being involved in support activities for Komeito which allows people to accumulate large quantities of religious virtue. O took this teaching seriously and was most active in outside activities. This woman, who had always put her husband first, had discovered a new path to self-realisation in Soka Gakkai activities. As soon as she came face to face she would talk about devotion, and when she heard talk of unhappiness or personal troubles, she would go out proselytising, even if it meant travelling long distances. When it came to election time, her eyes would fire up, and she would be out day and night.

As men usually worked during the day, election activities were mainly the work of the women's division. The power of the women's division at election time was amazing. They would gather together at a base point for each block, stand a name card with their candidate's name on a Buddhist altar, and then everyone would say the Nichiren prayer to pray for a decisive win. They would then take up Party publications and leaflets, and go around visiting friends and acquaintances to request their votes, not overlooking even the remotest of connections. No funds at all were provided for these activities by either Soka Gakkai or Komeito, so that members bore all travel and gift expenses themselves. However, because they believed that these election activities were worth the same religious merit as converting people, as they were also in accordance with the goals of *kosen rufu* and *obutsu myogo*, the members did not find them a burden. When their candidate was successfully elected they would fly into raptures and congratulate each other, saying "The achievements of men are due to the power of women."

A plan was put forward for collecting funds to erect a main hall at Taisekiji temple, and services for the dead were held to raise funds for the construction. The followers believed that by performing these services, religious merit accrued would be multiplied and returned to them, so they competed with each other and pushed themselves extra hard to make money to donate, amassing in a short time an amount of money that would have made ordinary people gasp in amazement. Even in S's house, O did things such as surrendering her insurance policy, gathering together and giving as much money as she could, leaving no ready cash. O's opinion was "We managed to accumulate enough religious merit to pull us out of our earlier terrible situation to bring us to where we are now, so I want to donate this money out of gratitude for this, and also to accumulate much more religious merit."

Shortly after, S's husband began to harbour the ambition to become a Soka Gakkai executive, and then soon after to stand for candidacy as a Diet member for Komeito. S was aware that O also shared her son's ambitions. More than a desire to rise to eminence and become famous, the attraction for him was the honour of carrying out the mission of *kosen rufu* and *obutsu myogo*.

The most important element in becoming an executive of Soka Gakkai is the accumulation of large numbers of converts. The husband used all his time after work and his holidays for Soka Gakkai activities and also went out proselytising, and O ultimately accredited all her converts to her son, so that their conversion would be marked up to him. Her son was soon appointed to an official post and went on to be promoted. He became an active party member when Komeito was inaugurated.

Finally he was nominated as a candidate in elections for members of the municipal assembly, and each day his home was like a battlefield. As voting day drew closer, he slept only three or four hours a night. On the day the ballots were counted, S saw on television a flash announcement that he had been elected; she felt immensely relieved, and immediately blacked out and collapsed.

Her husband now a Diet member, S became tangled up in his busy lifestyle. She had never been robust, and now as her fatigue accumulated, her physical state deteriorated, and following the next election she finally had to be admitted to hospital.

The husband had always been lord and master of the household, and was too lazy to ever lift a finger in the home. He was the type of man who was too embarassed to say a kind word to his wife, and even now he showed no consideration for her when she had collapsed from overwork. When he showed his face briefly at the hospital, complaining all the while of how busy he was, the only thing he could say his wife was "You have to chant the Nichiren prayer more strongly to get your strength back," openly demonstrating his dissatisfaction and annoyance at the inconvenience and hindrance he felt at his wife's hospitalisation.

S knew that complaining of being too busy was inexcusable in a Gakkai believer, but still she became inexplicably saddened. Unable to quell the urge to weep welling up inside her, she pulled the futon up over her head and wept silently at length. S began to analyze her situation:

"I believed that if I sincerely practiced as I was told to that I would undoubtedly find happiness, which is the reason for all my earnest efforts, despite which I can't say that I'm happy now."

"Ever since my husband was voted onto the Gakkai Central Executive Committee and then went on to become a Diet member, I have been sharing the burden of his increased duties and responsibilities. I always have to cut corners with the household budget to secure the extra funds to cover the increased financial burden that goes with his new status, so our lifestyle is certainly not one of luxury. A wife like me deserves more recognition for her assistance and support. Aren't the men just reaping the rewards of the hard work of the women? Aren't the women just being skilfully used by the organisation?"

The dissatisfaction she had been repressing began to surge up, and as thoughts she did not want to be thinking came to mind, S shook her head in confusion.

Upon reflection, Soka Gakkai was at its peak at around the time construction of the main hall was completed. Since then the organisation grew to massive proportions, and vast sums of money were changing hands when it was rocked by a succession of almost unbelievable scandals. S was shocked, and began to harbour doubts in her heart, despite which she was compelled to convey to those below her the directive handed down from above that said "What the mass media is reporting is nothing more than false rumors and malicious gossip. This is a scheme by people who wish to destroy the Gakkai and Komeito, so do not be misled. Do not look at, listen to or read anything other than the Seikyo Shinbun." Naturally neither criticism nor suspicions were permitted. S's hands were completely tied by the organisation.

K and G had been classmates at university. K was attracted to G, a tall, handsome and kind-natured young man. It was around the time G began to respond to K's positive approaches, that she discovered his whole family were Soka Gakkai members. His parents had been members for as far back as he could remember, making him what could be called a second-generation Soka Gakkai member.

"What! Soka Gakkai?" The image K had of Soka Gakkai up until that point had been of an organisation that was somehow questionable or weird, and so she was more than a little bewildered.

"If you feel you want to marry me, then it is important to me that you understand about Soka Gakkai." G set about putting K's preconceptions straight, stressing to her that Soka Gakkai was a modern organisation which focused on being anti-war and pro-peace and put its energies into cultural activities, differentiating it from older-style religious organisations. He enticed K out to all kinds of Gakkai functions; she saw art and photography exhibitions, experienced music and cultural festivals, and felt that certainly they did not reek of religion, and that on a cultural level too they were of quite a high standard. K was overwhelmed by some aspects of these activities, such as the enormity of the cultural festival, the dynamism and visual splendor of the human mosaic constructed to form the character for 'person', human pyramid by young female and male Gakkai members, and group dancing. Her attitude gradually began to change.

G took her to his home to meet his parents. His mother, A, was head of the local women's division, and while good-natured and sociable, was also overbearing - a typical Gakkai women's division type. K somehow felt that she would not be able to get along well with her, but she decided not too worry too much about it as they would not be living together.

After graduating from university, G entered a Gakkai-affiliated publishing company, and K found employment at the legal office of a lawyer who was a distant relative, and before long the two married, before which event K had already become a Gakkai member. It was spring of 1975.

The newly-wed couple rented an apartment and began their married life both working. After they began to live together, K was amazed that G made no effort to contribute, or rather was unable to do anything around the house. His mother had never disciplined him to do anything. A had always been a full-time housewife, and held the opinion that it was a housewife's mission in life to take care of her husband and children. Even when she was busy with Gakkai activities, she still never skimped on the housework. As head of the women's division, she also actively gave advice to the same effect.

K was dissatisfied that despite them being equally tired after a day at work, it was only she who did housework after arriving home.

Irritated, they fell to arguing. A commented lightly that if both of them working made things difficult then K should give up her job. "The key to peace and harmony in a household is the man going out to work and the wife protecting the home. This is the wisest way for a woman to live."

As head of the women's division, A was diligent in Gakkai activities such as discussion meetings and electoral activities, and fulfilling her financial obligations, and in order to support her teacher Ikeda Daisaku and Soka Gakkai activities, she needed her husband to be healthy, working well and earning money. That is why the first prerogative for the women's division is that they be good wives. A idolised Ikeda, always adding a comment about "teacher" to everything she said. "Teacher doesn't like women like that," or "teacher likes things like this," and so on, using "what teacher likes" as her standard for everything.

K had seen her own mother totally supported and become servile, always lamenting her lot, and was sure she did not want that kind of existence. Her opinion was that without economic strength, a woman could not be independent, so she wanted to continue working long after she was married.

K and G had rented an apartment about five minutes walk from G's mother, because A had said they should live as close as possible so she could help out with anything. However, she also wanted to be able to check on whether the young couple were neglecting their devotional activities.

A said that it was good that their households were now separate, and that K should order five copies each of the Seikyo Shinbun and the Komei Shinbun. When she had visited G's house before they were married, K had asked why there was such a large pile of newspapers from the same date of issue. In reply, A had said "The Seikyo Shinbun is a letter from the teacher. It's not just to read for yourself. Giving it to friends and acquaintances to read helps out with promulgation. Proceeds from newspaper sales are for promulgation of the teachings, and so also help your ancestors." At a discussion meeting one day, one member related how she was taking some expensive medicine which she had been told would be effective against the chronic disease she had, but it had not worked. A said to her "If you are going to spend so much money on paying for medicine, you should use that money to buy the Seikyo Shinbun. Your disease would certainly be healed then as a result of the religious merits you would accrue for services for repose of your ancestors." K couldn't believe her ears when she heard this.

Instructions had been passed down about "newspaper enlightenment." In other words there had been a message to increase newspaper sales, and the heads of each area and block were doing their best to achieve their quota. If the member's sickness had not healed even after doing exactly as she was told the issue would have been closed with the words "That's because your faith is weak."

Unable to go against his mother, G said to K, who had decided that one of each would be enough, that he would pay for them, and so it was decided that they would get three issues of each.

Even after coming home exhausted from work or on their days off, A would try to take the two of them with her to a discussion meeting, a counselling meeting or out on election activities. When she could only get G to go and K would not go, she would threaten them saying that if they neglected their Gakkai activities they would see no good results. One day at a discussion meeting they had reluctantly attended, the head of the senior division was giving a talk detailing some actual examples of how important a wife's support and assistance was to a man. K became irritated as she listened, and was unable to refrain from voicing her indignation. "Why do the men always have to be supported? I want to see the women get some support." The head of the senior division, despite an expression indicating she had been momentarily caught off guard, responded "men are useless if they are not supported. You know that don't you?" Immediately the whole room broke out in laughter. Unable to bear it any longer, K rose from her seat. Her body was trembling with humiliation and rage.

K had already decided how she was going to use her bonus and was looking forward to it. However, G told her that she should put it towards paying for services for her ancestors, and so they argued. A also said to her "You usually don't participate much in Gakkai activities, so at least you should make a hefty contribution to services for your ancestors." K replied, "I'm not earning money for Soka Gakkai. I'm earning it to use for myself" to which A responded with a sigh, "You don't understand the first thing about devotion."

And what is devotion? Properly speaking, faith is something which should lead to the attainment of a free and unfettered heart, but it seems that in the Soka Gakkai faith, freedom of the heart is, on the contrary, lost as a result of coercive control and supervision. Despite all her efforts, K was unable to keep up with the system of ideas and thoughts peculiar to Gakkai members. All good was the result of virtue, while all bad was the result of sin. This two-dimensional theory of virtue and sin was all reduced to faith. The idea of "sin" was also not based on some consciousness of wrongdoing arrived at through introspection or reflection, but the receiving of punishment for a lack of faith or for reviling the Buddhist teachings. A lack of enthusiasm for Gakkai activities or election activities, or even the slightest criticism, and you were threatened with punishment. Doubts or suspcions were deemed the evil of the self; criticism was labelled as one of the seven kinds of pride, considering oneself to be more worthy or virtuous than one actually is; a lack of faith was reviling the Buddhist teaching; and a lack of understanding and criticism from outside was labelled as the three hindrances and the four evils, so that all were interpreted into fearful Buddhist terminology.

K had fallen in love with G, becoming a Gakkai member in order that she could build a happy married life with him, but now this faith was causing conflict and discord, and a gulf was appearing between them. Forced into this dilemma, K was very troubled. She had lost confidence in her married life with G when she discovered that she was pregnant. Despite her dismay, not having the heart to go through with an abortion, she decided to have the baby, giving birth to a girl.

As a mother, K tasted a fullness in her life she had never known before. She felt a rush of love every time she put her baby to her breast. As she softly caressed that cheek with her finger, fine and delicate like a petal, smooth like silk, she felt a new desire surge up within her to live a good and wholesome life in order to properly look after and raise this little life.

It was on a day K was enjoying her new motherhood that she opened a page of a weekly magazine to notice an article about Soka Gakkai, catching her breath when she saw the photograph there. A middle-aged overweight man had a pretty young girl seated on his lap, and was writing circles and crosses on her face with a marker pen. The overweight man was unmistakably Ikeda Daisaku. Standing around him were four or five top members of the Executive Council, watching and laughing. It was an unbelievable scene. As she gazed at this scene, indescribable feelings of repulsion and rage welled up inside her. Here was Ikeda doodling on the soft pure skin of a child as if desecrating it. Such behaviour could not be considered normal, no matter how you looked at it. When she thought that it could be her own child being scribbled on like this, she quivered with anger. In an almost murderous rage, she wanted to knock him down. She also felt disgusted with the men at his side watching and laughing. If Ikeda was doing it, no matter what it might be, they would follow him and laugh. K had the feeling she had caught a glimpse of the real nature of Soka Gakkai. It was improbable that Ikeda would have behaved in such a way in front of anyone from outside, which meant that a close attendant who had been present at the time had taken the photograph and leaked it outside, and then it had made its way into a weekly magazine. That act itself also smelled somewhat sinister.

Around that time a number of members of the Chief Executive Council began to rebel against the organisation in succession, making public accusations. People such as A held that anyone who turned against Ikeda was a wicked person whose faith had become twisted, but the shock within the Gakkai was inconcealable. For rebels to appear even with strict control and supervision, meant that there were also problems in the higher ranks, and looking at the photograph, K had the feeling she understood why.

That photograph served to confirm K's suspicions about Ikeda Daisaku and Soka Gakkai. There was no way she could follow the religion now. K decided to leave the organisation, a departure which finally led to her divorce. G was perplexed as he had not intended to part with K, but he was unable to leave with her. K took her child and went home to her parents. The divorce was a serious blow to her, but released from the spell of the organisation, K breathed freely for the first time in some time, taking the first step on a new road to independence.

7. Troubled Women

More than anything else, O looked forward to paying her respects at the head temple Soka Gakkai members referred to as "the temple." Both her heart and body were refreshed by a walk through the groves of dense ancient cryptomerias in the vast temple grounds of Taisekiji, which looks up onto Mt. Fuji from its position at the mountain's base. O was proud of her meritorious donation of funds for the construction of the main hall, despite the strain on her personal finances. She was always overcome with wonder and joy when she entered the magnificent chalkstone main hall, built in the shape of a crane spreading its wings, and came into the presence of the main image located at the rear of the dazzling golden altar. For O, this was her spiritual home.

Soka Gakkai is known as a group of devotees who supports the Nichiren sect's main temple, Taisekiji, from outside the sect, and photographs often appear in Soka Gakkai publications of President Ikeda smiling and chatting with the abbot of Taisekiji, a beautiful picture of harmony between monk and layman. O always viewed those photographs with a feeling of gratitude, without the slightest notion of the discord which had existed between the Gakkai and its parent sect for some years, never even suspecting such things. It was a shock to O when the conflict between the two men, remaining unresolved, gradually escalated to the point where finally they began to criticise each other publicly.

She did not understand who had done what to whom, but all she could do was to pray earnestly that this was just a temporary difference of opinion, that it would be amicably settled as soon as possible, and that the status quo would be restored. However this was not to be, and eventually the Gakkai were excommunicated by the parent sect. The Seikyo Shinbun carried articles daily attacking the parent sect, and the instructions "Don't visit your neighborhood temple. Don't call Buddhist priests to your funerals. Carry out your funerals using either Soka Gakkai or your friends." What on earth was going on?

O could not imagine her devotions without the parent sect. Not to be able to visit "the temple," which had been her biggest joy, would be the saddest thing of all. Over eighty years of age, O felt that if she could not have priests chant at her funeral that she would not be able to reach Nirvana. All her devotions to date had been in vain. As she chanted the Nichiren prayer, tears ran down her face. Troubled beyond words, no longer able to think, O finally decided to leave the Gakkai and join the parent sect.

Her son, understanding his mother's feelings at having few years remaining, was unable to oppose her decision. S could not say anything either. In consideration of her son's position, O left the house and went to live with her oldest daughter. As she passes her remaining years, visiting "the temple" is her only joy.

S was envious of the way her mother-in-law was conducting herself in accordance with her own heart. Observing the wrangle between the parent sect and the Gakkai, followers attacking each other with foul words and abusive language, she felt sad and miserable, and felt she could not bear it. She had no desire to judge which side was right or which was wrong. She began to feel nihilistic, wanted to totally escape from this world, but she couldn't do that either.

Unable to prevent his mother from leaving the Gakkai, O's son's responsibility as an executive was under question, and he was gravely perplexed.

Divorced by K and unable to live by himself, G returned to live with his mother. G was badly shaken. Grieved by the split with K, he lapsed into depression, in addition to which one of his close friends from his university days had left the Gakkai. G began to publicly criticise Soka Gakkai. A was desperate to do the right thing to support her son and to get him back on his feet. Believing in Ikeda, never doubting him, A harbored rage and hatred for the parent sect. Surely it was the great deeds of her teacher Ikeda that had led Nichiren Shoshu to its current heights of prosperity, creating such a magnificent main temple. To then go and excommunicate Ikeda was absurd. Now that such a thing had happened, she would remain faithful to Ikeda to the last, her only option being to do battle with the Soka Gakkai against the parent sect. She made the grim resolution not to look back.

8. Where is the Renaissance?

Soka Gakkai dislikes being categorised as a "new religion," boasting instead of its status as a group of devotees of the Nichiren Shoshu temple, Taisekiji, with a tradition spanning back seven hundred years and a legitimate teaching lineage stretching back directly to Nichiren himself. This itself is true, and unlike the founder of Aum Shinrikyo, Shoko Asahara, or the founder of The Institute for Research in Human Happiness, Ryuho Okawa, Ikeda Daisaku is not a founder, but rather just another believer (recently he is not even accorded that status).

Soka Gakkai is an officially-recognised religion, but this recognition was accorded on the basis of observance of three conditions laid down by the parent sect, Nichiren Shoshu, as follows:

1. Converted believers must belong to a Nichiren Shoshu temple.
2. Doctrine of the head temple must be upheld.
3. Respect for the Three Treasures (Buddha, Dharma and Sangha).

Therefore, no matter how powerful the Gakkai may become, they can never be anything more than followers of Nichiren Shoshu. This is Soka Gakkai's stumbling block.

Now that the Gakkai has been expelled from the main temple and has lost its grounds for authority, what road will it take in the future? The organisation continues its fierce aggressive campaign against Nichiren Shoshu, energetically propagandising that the Gakkai is the righteous mainstream, that this is the era of Buddhism for the masses, for the renaissance of the Soka Gakkai and the renaissance of Buddhism. Meanwhile, rumour has it that the hall under construction in Hachioji is going to be the new head temple for the launching of "Ikedaism." However, if that is the case, what is to become of the main image? The main image located in the main hall of Taisekiji at Mt. Fuji ought to be the basic object of the Soka Gakkai faith. Within the Soka Gakkai, it seems word is going around that if the current high priest of the Nichiren sect, Nikken, and his supporters were purged and someone different were to succeed him, that the Gakkai could come to friendly terms with Nichiren Shoshu, and the status quo could be restored. However, this would mean yielding to the power of the parent sect, presumably placing the Soka Gakkai under its jurisdiction.

The worst victims of the Gakkai-Shoshu strife are the Soka Gakkai members themselves. No one is more distressed than earnest Gakkai followers. But while they are also distressed, those members of the women's division who are such obedient devotees of Ikeda will once again easily be carried along in whichever direction the Gakkai may go.

There is a series of publications called "Women's Renaissance." Anticipating perhaps some new vision, a glance reveals nothing more than a collection of testimonies from women's division members across the country saying how wrong Nichiren Shoshu was in its actions or how corrupt and degenerate are its priests.

The objective of the so-called "renaissance," so enthusiastically touted in recent times by the Gakkai, remains unclear. Is it an attempt to substitute the current Gakkai position for the Christian religious revolution of the Middle Ages, or to liken Ikeda Daisaku to Martin Luther? It seems more to be a low level attack on Nichiren Shoshu.

Based on the Buddhist concept of respect for life, Soka Gakkai and the Komeito strongly advocate an anti-war, pro-peace position, and have actively sponsored a range of activities in line with this. As such, leaving aside the religious aspect, Komeito has also enjoyed the support of the aware public who have held them in high regard as a force for peace. The core of that force for peace is (or should have been) the women's division. The Komeito of recent times has politically edged closer to the Liberal Democratic Party, and despite explanations of such actions as "negotiation" or "cultivating good relations," the reality has been full co-operation in formulating the PKO legislation. Far from opposing this, the women's division went around during the election activities for the Upper House which followed advocating that Komeito's acceptance of the bill as it stood was correct.

In the Upper House election of July 1992, the low voter turnout worked in Komeito's favor, and the party upset all expectations to emerge victorious. After the sense of danger resulting from the enormous shakeup over the conflict with the parent sect, Soka Gakkai tossed aside their usual line about the separation of religion and politics, and under the grand command of Ikeda Daisaku, the whole organisation campaigned furiously for the election. Word even spread that sumo wrestler Mitoizumi had hoisted the Gakkai flag on his victory parade. As a result, Komeito managed to capture more votes than in the previous election, increasing their number of parliamentary seats, and showing the Gakkai to be a powerful electoral force. The bigger the social and political influence of the Soka Gakkai and the Komeito becomes, the more this trend will draw attention.

Electoral victory brought Soka Gakkai renewed confidence, and it can be anticipated that this attitude will show in its future dealings with Nichiren Shoshu. Even as a former Gakkai member, I want to close my eyes and block my ears to the Asura-like constant fighting of organisation as a whole, which drags in all the members and is the biggest obstacle to faith, and the supply of low level news items to weekly magazines. If the Soka Gakkai is truly a religious organisation, then it should remove itself as quickly as possible from the ugly battle in which it is engaged, so that the hearts of members can be left to peace to carry out their religious devotions with joy.

Victims of the Emperor Faith

Chun Kwangne

1. Listening to the Voices of Korean Women

As a Korean woman in Japan, the comfort women problem has presented me with many difficult questions, raising as it does issues of racial and sexual discrimination. About 15 or 16 years ago I first came across the book "The Comfort Women" (Japanese), but was unable at that stage to confront this knowledge head on. Naturally the contents shocked me, but it was not simply lack of courage that held me back from wanting to know more, at the time I was struggling with my own inner turmoil over the history and treatment of Koreans in Japan, and did not want to know more about the comfort women because having to identify with them in any way would burden me with the knowledge of the intolerable sexual abuse they suffered. My impulse was to escape from this knowledge. I wanted to accept myself as a Korean woman, and it was not possible for me to complicate the issue by confronting directly the existence of comfort women - the acme of racial and sexual discrimination.

For a long time I was caught up with my own problems of identity, and was only vaguely aware of the ideology and disputes of fellow countrymen regarding issues such as forced labourers, the Korean war, the split of Korea and the struggle for democracy and unification. Although I was envious of those who grappled with important racio-political problems, I continued to be confused and unable to move. However much I tried to learn more about history and the current situation, it only added to the confusion, and so I gave up all thought of reading books with titles such as "Comfort Women" or "Forced Labourers."

More than ten years passed, and one day the comfort women issue again came to my notice. This time my reaction was different; I felt such a shock, as if my blood were running backwards. I recalled my previous ineffectiveness but did not have time to fall into self-despair, for I was already reaching for the telephone to contact fellow Koreans tackling this issue.

In retrospect, the problems of my own confused heart and the comfort women, were born of a common historical process and structure. The large Korean population resident in Japan and the existence of comfort women, are both the direct result of Japanese colonisation of Korea in the name of the Emperor. The origins of both, therefore, can be said to lie in the Emperor system, which was supported by imperialists before the war, and essentially maintained unchanged by conservative powers afterwards. Involvement in the comfort women issue was for me, an attempt to clear the confusion which had weighed on me for so long. Only very recently have I gained the confidence to a reaffirm my identity as a 2.5 generation Korean woman in Japan.[1] The starting point of my liberation as such, must lie in facing up to the realities of the pain the comfort women suffered. Not only this, by listening to the voices of the long-ago first generation of men and women who endured such bitter experiences, a picture of my oppressed self might emerge and I can open up the hidden pain to investigate the root causes and dismantle the hurt. I believed that I would be able to discover a new self that demands liberation.

And so at last I joined with other Korean women who had long been involved in the struggle for recognition and justice for former comfort women. One night after a long meeting had finally finished, I went to a bar with two other women for a drink. We said cheers over a cool beer, and then one woman muttered, "It's taken nearly fifty years hasn't it, to start finding out the facts and working on a solution." We all sighed and were silent. That moment left a deep impression on me. In the silence that followed I think we were each reflecting on our family history and struggles as Korean women in Japan.

---

[1] My father was a first generation Korean in Japan and my mother was second generation. Accordingly my father used to say I was second generation and my mother that I was third generation, hence I decided to call myself 2.5 generation.

On August 15th 1945 - a day I do not consider as 'Liberation Day' - the Koreans dispersed throughout Japan were ignored, and did not receive a single word of apology from Emperor Hirohito or Prime Minister Kantaro Suzuki. Formerly the 'Emperor's babies,' the treatment meted out to the first generation of Koreans who had been regarded as Japanese, was tantamount to that of disposable rags. It was difficult for them to even find the boat fare to return home, and they had to rebuild their lives again from nothing and unaided.

During the Korean War, scrap iron collected by the first generation was ironically turned into weapons which endangered the lives of their relatives in Korea. Wives who had had to stow away in ships to come to Japan in search of husbands rounded up in Korea as forced labor, were treated by the Japanese authorities as illegal immigrants and arrested as criminals. There were many hardships for this first generation who had no choice in the circumstances but to stay on in Japan, or those who came back looking for work when there was none in Korea. They were poor and weak from lack of food, and subject to unrelenting prejudice and discrimination from ordinary Japanese citizens, with whom they were certainly not allowed to live or work on an equal footing. Consequently, they were pushed into places like riverbeds and marshes to live, where they built barrack houses and lived cheek to cheek. Doing the lowest paid, menial work and living in a poor environment, somehow they eked out a living to bring up the second generation.

There are still cases even now where Koreans are forced to evacuate from the riversides where they had long-lived, without being offered a single yen in compensation from the Ministry of Construction. There are many examples of people being evicted and scattering without leaving a trace. The struggles of the first generation in particular have been, to borrow a phrase the Japanese government has repeatedly used, "beyond description."

My own grandmother could not marry according to her feelings. She crossed the Sea of Genkai in her teens to marry my grandfather, of whom she had not even seen a picture. Men who were brought by force to Japan or came in search of work had trouble finding marriage partners, and so it was common to marry hometown relatives, or through acquaintance's connections. No sooner had young Korean women come out to Japan to marry in the turmoil before and after WWII, than they were put to work doing heavy labour. It was not surprising that families of the first-generation Koreans should break up under the tightly regulated life, and the deep-rooted contempt for Koreans evident in the daily prejudice endured by the men. Under these circumstances, my grandmother had to deal with housework, shopping and child-rearing, and take on side jobs as well in order to feed the children being born one after another. She continued to make illicit alcohol while under continual threat of crackdown by the police, but was never once caught. I can imagine her lining up the children with hands tightly clasped in front of the cupboard where the moonshine was hidden, feigning innocence in answer to the policeman's questions.

The men raised pigs and sometimes earned cash from work unloading at the docks, but there was never any stability in their daily lives. Many daily labourers lived in places with not even enough space for work-exhausted men to lie flat, and would work at a machine all day without getting a decent amount of sleep at night. For women who had only received a colonial education about the Emperor in their home country, or had no education at all, buying a ticket by themselves and even getting on a train was a daunting task. Once when I went to the meeting of a certain new religion, my grandmother asked me to write her name for her on the back of the donation envelope.

I have never stopped regretting that at the time, it didn't even occur to me to wonder why the older women couldn't read or write their own names. I never listened to stories of the old people's troubles, which went in one ear and out the other, and recoil at the thought of my egotistical self who saw (or rather didn't want to see) their hardship stories and complaints as no more than idle grumbling. Reflecting now on the escapist and cold-hearted self who ignored their pain, I have to make a clean breast of it - no excuses - and record how much I despised, looked down on, and distanced myself from them.

The lives of those women, some of whom were forced to be comfort women, could be the stuff of a great novel. In Japan they lived under the sexually discriminating structures of patriarchy and confucianism. They were responsible everyday for housework, child-rearing, labour and looking after their husband, father-in-law and mother-in-law. If they ventured one step outside the house, then consciousness of the imperialistic patriarchal system was absorbed, and the deeply-rooted imperialist mentality of Japanese society stood in their way to exclude and discriminate against them.

The division of the mother country also caused splits in families and Korean society in Japan. In contrast to the Korean desire for togetherness, the situation compelled families to split, producing a deep schism in human relations. The bitterness my grandmother feels at having to part from sons and daughters whom she may never see again if there is no unification, can never be allayed.

2. Asian Women and Japanese Men's Sexuality

Ever since former comfort woman Kim Hak Sun decided to file a suit demanding compensation and an apology from the Japanese government, a succession of Korean women have come to Japan. As the debate increased, the women's voices and the Japanese government's defense were reported at the same time in many countries across the Pacific. In Canada where I live at present, there are many enquiries ascertaining the authenticity of the governments apology and investigation report. The atrocities committed by the Japanese military are unparalleled in history, and the number of people concerned about the Japanese government's handling of these matters after the war has certainly increased, and is not just confined to citizens of Japanese or Korean descent.

Koreans were not the only comfort women, and when it came to light that women from six Asian countries were also victims, the expression of one Filipina friend I was with at the time I heard this, became set in a pained look. It was not simply the comfort women she was thinking of, but also the so-called 'Japanyukis,' women coming to Japan to find work and being forced into prostitution, and the groups of Japanese men going to the Phillipines on sex tours. The situation of these Asian women in Japan could be called the latest version of the comfort women. Industry has taken over from where the former Japanese Imperial Army left off, wielding money and economic power in place of bayonets and military might. Japanese men are using up Asian women both in and outside Japan as though they are simply merchandise; in the past they were regarded as war supplies, now they are sexual commodities forced to be communal receptacles for Japanese men. And the men who go shopping for women, show no sign whatsoever of any sense of guilt.

Such behaviour is aggression towards Asia in a different form; the result of Japan's non-recognition of its history of aggression in Asia, neglect of the facts behind the apologies and compensation, and lack of history and human rights education based on a searching of the conscience. The apparent lack of guilt over the continuing exploitation of Asian women, is due to the fact that there has been no deep soul-searching on the comfort women issue, which has been all but ignored. This exploitation, which could be called the acme of racial and sexual discrimination, is now being recreated in a different guise by the generation of descendants of Japanese soldiers.

Former Japanese soldiers grieve for comrades who died in the war and visit old battle sites every year to search for remains of the dead, but how many of them shed a single tear over the people of the Pacific islands and Asian countries who were victims of Japanese aggression. How many former soldiers remember the comfort women who were left behind to meet a tragic end on the battlefields. They received a pension from the Japanese government after the war, but complained about their taxes being raised two or three times in order to compensate Asian victims of the war. Such people do not pass on reflections and a sense of culpability to their children and grandchildren, and so it is natural for a new aggression to arise from their grandsons' generation.

Young Japanese going on overseas trips exchange information on prostitution at their destinations, and many times I have witnessed small groups sallying out into the nightlife districts. I have been present at places where they select a sex partner and boast about how many local women they had sex with and how much they paid. After returning home the very first thing such young people do is rush to have a check-up for venereal diseases, and recently AIDS checks as well. The really shocking thing is the reaction of their girlfriends who listen with deep interest to stories of prostitution without so much as even raising a protest. It ought to be borne in mind that they are undoubtedly the generation of grandchildren of former Japanese soldiers.

In 1991 I heard of a Japanese woman around the same age as me, who hid contraceptives in her husband's suitcase whenever he went on a business trip in Asia. If it were an affair with a Japanese woman then it would be cause for jealousy, but if a husband buys an Asian woman for sex then it is seen only from a rationalist point of view. Far from questioning her husband's warped morality and sexuality, this woman did not even notice that she had become an accomplice in the crime by promoting it. Recently the prejudice that Asian women are the source of AIDS infection is also on the increase.

To give an example: Asian women workers in all regions of Japan have been experiencing trouble for some time, but this came to a head at a public bathhouse where the manager was pressured over which customers to allow entry, by a regular customer who said "If they [Asian descent foreigners] are using the same bath then I won't come. Even if they don't have AIDS, you don't know what diseases they've got." Despite already being in an uncertain position business-wise, the manager apparently finally sent a letter of apology to the regular customer saying, "Public baths are something that people who have no bath cannot be deprived of."

This account shows just how Asian women, who are sacrificed as an outlet for Japanese men's sexual desire, are easily seen as a source of AIDS contamination. Regarding them as unclean in addition to lusting after their bodies, robs them of value as human beings. Comfort women and Asian women are the ones who are the victims, and it is their own shameful conduct as human beings that Japanese men ought to be making an issue of.

Put another way, the influence of contemporary Japan was behind the exchange between the regular customer and public bath manager, and which of the two roads selected was of symbolic importance. Whatever the manager's views on Japan's past relations with Asia may have been, he was at least not wavered by warped prejudices and determined to live together with Asians residing in Japan. In doing so, he brushed away the distorted pre-war view of Asians, which suggests that living together with Asian people is the first step along the road to internationalisation. The customer on the other hand, was still peddling an unchanged pre-war view of Asian people, in pressing for discrimination and exclusion. This is an apt exposure of the reality behind the belief in a post-war Japan of 'peace and democracy.'

In Kawaskai where I lived until 1991, there was a comparatively large population of workers from Asia. One day when I attended a women's neighbourhood meeting, the topic of Asian workers and residents came up. Almost all the people there knew that I was a 2.5 generation Korean using only a Korean name, but this fact did not cause them to be reserved in their comments. Perhaps it is because I was born in Japan, speak the language like a Japanese and have two children by a Japanese husband, that I felt that I was regarded as being of a higher class than other Asian workers. These ladies in their fifties are usually kind, but when it came to the topic of Asian residents in the neighbourhood they became quite indignant, with comments like, "It's troubling isn't it, public morals will be corrupted," and so on. Then the talk continued on the subject of how people coming from Asia disturb public order, which not one person disputed. At that time there was much talk of the wedding of Prince Akishino and a 'Kiko-san boom' was in full swing. So of course when the conversation turned to this, their views were the exact opposite of those on Asian women; the talk was only of the standards of nobility, purity and beauty in the Imperial family. I returned home in a dark mood having had reconfirmed how deep the roots of discrimination are, in a structure with the Emperor at its apex.

In the process of coming to grips with the comfort women issue, many aspects of their history arose which could not be ignored. One in particular which made me think, was the former comfort women who hid themselves away, keeping their past secret and leading lonely lives, or those who took their own lives out of shame.

Survivors who made public the fact they were former comfort women are reported to have become recluses or have obsessions with cleanliness. One woman who died in Okinawa in 1991, cut herself off from the world and lived, in spite of many inconveniences, in a small isolated hut behind a sugar cane field. After her death I saw a programme about her on television. It felt as if I were seeing the scars of the deep wounds in this woman's heart, in her old pot polished like new.

There is also a woman who has lived in Thailand ever since the war because she believes her body is not worthy to step on the soil of her native land again, and wherever she goes always carries a handkerchief and roll of tissues. Her living room contains a small Korean flag and a photograph of her mother. She told a Japanese journalist "I was married at the Lotus Flower Temple because I wanted to be reborn as the beautiful fragrant lotus which grows out of muddy water."[2] Her wounds, and those of others like her, are still not healed.

In spite of the humiliation of going public with the fact they were comfort women, and having to visit Japan in order to demand an apology and compensation from the Japanese government, the number of former Korean comfort women attempting to come to Japan is increasing. Only very recently women entering the courts dressed in sunglasses and wigs have been reported prominently. Even if these women did want to use their own names, it would be very difficult because of the stigma attached to comfort women and the effect it could have on the marriage prospects of children and grandchildren. And even if there are no children, if it were merely known that a family member had been a comfort woman, then that family name would be dishonoured. In 1991 at a gathering to hear the testimony of

---

2   Watashitachiwa Wasurenai - Chosenjin Jugunianfu, Zainichi Doho Josei no Kai.

women who had come to Japan, one woman's words showed how much she was ashamed of herself when she said, "I have made such a shameful display of myself," but the reaction of many present was that it is the Japanese soldiers who are shameful.

If these women - who were forced to become comfort women - are regarded as 'shameful' or 'unclean', then we are committing the crime of degrading them a second time. I believe that until the stigma is removed and thoughts of 'shameful' or 'unclean' are banished, a genuine resolution is impossible, and they will pass the remainder of their years in loneliness. The situation must be reversed by receiving support from the perpetrator of their unhappiness, the Japanese government, to return to their hometowns without shame and pass the rest of their lives.

Fundamental changes to my own passive and distorted view of sexuality are also necessary. If the source of ideas and mechanisms which have oppressed women up to now by creating and reproducing discrimination, stems from not only the Emperor system but patriarchy and confucianism as well, then we must come to grips with them. At the same time as the systems of religion and ideas are examined, it is also necessary to maintain a parallel struggle to surmount them, because even if a political solution is attained, as long as there is no reform in attitudes towards these women, they can never go back to their hometowns to spend the remainder of their lives with family and relatives.

One day in 1991 I saw an Asahi TV documentary about the comfort women. There was one scene in particular which riveted me. In answer to the question from the Japanese woman interviewer, "Have you ever thought about marriage," the former comfort woman fixed her with a steely eye for a second and answered. "Women who were comfort women aren't seen as human beings you know. Marriage? If you have a conscience there is no way you could do it with this body. I haven't ever even thought about it. What would I do if I got married? Do you think I could have children?" My heart was pierced by the sight of this woman fighting back tears after the interview and desperately wanted to ask why she said, "if you have a conscience."

These women's only life has been sacrificed and they are now not even treated as human beings. My blood boils when I think of them caught between the twin yokes of racial and sexual discrimination, while the person who bears the greatest responsibility for their suffering, Emperor Hirohito, enjoyed life and denied all blame. The woman's reply to the interviewer is in fact a serious question for fellow Koreans and Japanese. One that we must rise up to.

3. Easy Solidarity is not Possible

How do Japanese women interested in feminism see the relation between the comfort women issue, resident Korean women in Japan and Asian women? When I first started grappling with the issue of comfort women, I believed that we could form solidarity with Japanese feminists, but then I heard the following statement from one woman: "I have already heard enough of discrimination against Koreans by Japanese," and she then went on to say that from now on she would like to work together as women discriminated against by men, and with problems in common. In short it was a proposal to give 'the female point of view' greater importance as the meeting point of solidarity.

I must admit that in the past I have not responded very sensitively to discrimination against women, because for me the problems and anguish arising from being a Korean in Japanese society were much more pressing issues on a daily basis. I thought that the gap between myself and this woman might be due to my lack of understanding because I had not 'studied' feminism. But I felt that there was also a basic difference between us in the circumstances of our daily lives, which for her meant housework was neatly divided up with her husband (and that is certainly a desirable thing), and for me a situation where such a division could never be maintained as a rule.

Thinking through her proposal again and with this gap in mind, I began to sense the risks of solidarity; the reason being, she had already heard enough criticism of Japanese by Korean women, but sexual discrimination by Korean men against Korean women is inexorably bound up with this. As the result of oppression and discrimination forced on Koreans by Japanese society, the men's frustrations and irritations are vented in the form of discrimination against Korean women, and there is no escaping the fact that Japanese men *and* women, constitute a society which coordinates discrimination. I could not help feeling distrust of this woman's statement, because I know all too well the pain of Korean men in Japan, especially the first generation brought here by force, and second generation of my older brother.

I am fully aware that sexual discrimination between compatriots ought not to be tolerated, however, there are no common grounds for solidarity as long as it is not recognised that Korean residents of Japan are oppressed by Japanese men and women. It is impossible for me as a Korean woman in Japan to cut myself in two and separate the 'woman' from the 'Korean.' I felt that this proposal to define the problem by separating race and sex, brought with it the risk of splitting myself anew, and I could not endure to be divided any more than I already have. Therefore I could not bring myself to place my trust in a feminism and proposal for solidarity which would take the bones out of the oppression between races, and the conflicts and historical awareness of the oppressed. The 'liberation' I desire is a different one to this. Even if Japanese feminists did win the 'male and female' battle, to me that would mean nothing more than one oppressor changed for another wearing a skirt.

A true solidarity would be for Japanese women and Korean women residents of Japan to clarify positions on their racial and historical connections, and then come to grips with them through critical self-searching in order to accept our own responsibility. The potential for a solidarity could then emerge. I would not want the original purpose of an appeal from Japanese women to be forgotten, so that it would end up as another case of exploitation of the weak by the strong. Reflecting further, I resolved not to be seduced by the temptation to camouflage myself with the vices of the strong, and find myself being demeaned again.

4. The Emperor System and Christianity

As the comfort women issue indicates, in seeking a resolution to the various conflicts that have accumulated between Japan and various Asian countries, the very important issues of Emperor Hirohito's war responsibility and continuation of the Emperor system itself should not be overlooked. But there is still no sign of a proper settlement to the historical problem of Asian victims of Japanese aggression, and meanwhile a new invasion of Asia continues in various guises. Non-settlement of the comfort women issue and the prostitution problem with Asian countries described previously, are graphic manifestations of this.

For Koreans in Japan the spectre of a new aggression in Asia is axiomatic with coerced opppression through discrimination. Their pain stands alongside that of other minorities and those who are marginalised in Japanese society, and people who have felt the hurt of discrimination do not want to experience it again. Therefore to avoid repetition of such experiences, the basic causes of discrimination must be investigated and removed.

Korean residents in Japan stand where they are today having been subjected to all possible discrimination, and I am constantly amazed when confronted with each new incident, at the cruel discriminatory mentality concealed within Japanese citizens who normally seem good-natured. There is discrimination when trying to find a house, job or get married; from childhood until old age the prejudices of Japanese society are flung at us throughout our whole lives. Nearly fifty years since the war ended, various movements against discrimination have developed, and it could be said that the situation is improving, but a fundamental change in awareness is still a long way off.

Contempt of Asians and discrimination against them on a daily basis is rampant; with numerous 'incidents' and few examples of solutions. During the 7 years I was a member of the congregation of a small church in a Korean district in Kawasaki, about half the daily telephone calls I received were about incidents of discrimination, or if not, then about problems with no solution.

In the summer of 1990 a Korean woman friend of mine was turned down for a job because of her Korean nationality. It was her sixth refusal on such grounds from Japanese industry, and when I had lunch with her the next day she could not hold back her anger. I had often heard of such cases before, but on this particular occasion I was unable to stop myself from going straight to the company. I met the person in charge of the interviews and confirmed that Korean nationality was the reason for my friend being refused employment. A few days later I submitted a proposal to my Church Social Committee for an inquiry into, and resolution of this incident of racial prejudice. In the end the company admitted the fact of discrimination, apologised and decided to employ her. What is more, beginning the following year, human rights education for employees was held on a monthly basis. It consisted of mainly listening to talks and discussing Japanese and Korean modern history, and the history and situation of Koreans in Japan.

I'd like to mention the words of the company president at the time. "There are few chances for direct association with Korean residents of Japan. I think the prejudices we hold against them are probably a result of the education received from the time we are children. During the war and colonisation, we had the sense of feeling superior. Receiving such mistaken education, we swallowed it all down." ('Toitsu Nippo,' 15th December, 1990).

This company president's words clearly illustrate the reason for Japanese people's prejudice towards Koreans. Namely, an imperialist mentality and history of colonialism before the war, which has continued down to the present day with no searching of the conscience or improvements.

Whenever we are confronted with any kind of discrimination, it seems that dominating the consciousness of those Japanese people who do discriminate, is the Emperor. Whether consciously or unconsciously, the pull of the 'Emperor Faith' on Japanese people is very powerful. Furthermore, through the concept of being separate from Asia to be part of Europe, prejudice against Asian people was sanctioned and a discriminatory mentality was consolidated. This mentality and way of thinking has not been eradicated, and in a situation where it is resurging if anything, what can people with any religion be thinking of?

I was baptised because I wanted to be liberated from the yoke of discrimination against Koreans in Japanese society, and from the Confucian ethics of Korean society within Japan. It was a pity, however, that I could not find what I was looking for at the Japanese theological school I entered after being baptised. At the Tokyo Union Theological Seminary, studies of negro theology, feminist theology or the folk theology born in Korea (which certainly had relevance for my situation), were considered just fashions, and there was if anything a tendency to avoid theology which approached the issue of human liberation. The subject and situation of people oppressed historically and politically in Japanese society, was avoided as a political and social problem.

In 1967 the Japan Church of Christ to which I belonged, made a Confession of War Responsibility admitting and apologising for the invasion of Asia and crimes committed during WWII, and entreating God's forgiveness. Originally Japan had invaded Asia and inflicted intolerable persecution in Korea, starting with enforced Shinto worship. This Confession of War Responsibility was an admission of willing cooperation in historical crimes committed during the invasion of Asia, and is a resolve as Christians, not to repeat them. It is concrete proof that an admission of guilt is taken seriously and bears witness to a way of living. As such, it signifies a strong connection with the situation of Asian victims and their descendants, who are still suffering and for whom the scars will not heal. But at the Church of Christ Tokyo Union Theological Seminary, I did not once hear about the important significance of the Confession of War Responsibility, or the historical background in any affirmative or positive sense.

At the time the Confession of War Responsibility was made public during the 1970s, problems with the world expositions held in Osaka and Okinawa, and conflict at the Tokyo Union Theological Seminary were continuing.[3] The post-war history of the Japanese Church of Christ is significant to the lives of Koreans in Japan, because it parallels the history of relations with various countries of Asia who were victims of aggression, and is also the history of relations with a nation having an emperor system. As long as the history of these relations is not properly comprehended, both 'love of one's neighbours' and 'peace' will not follow. Mission work and proselytism based on a theology, gospel and faith that cannot eliminate an imperialist mentality or the concept of belonging to Europe not Asia, and which lacks a historical understanding based on facts, will only produce a new discrimination based on an imperialist mentality.

One fellow Christian woman came to consult me after she had gone to a Japanese Church; the moment she spoke her mother tounge there, she was reproved with "Don't speak Korean here." She is now not attending any church. In the colonial education system taught in the name of the emperor, Koreans were forbidden to speak in their mother tounge, and now history repeats itself through the church.

Even in a mission school I once heard a truly astonishing statement. In 1990 at a mission school assembly on the theme of 'Living Together,' I gave a talk about the history of relations between Japan and Korea and the current situation of Koreans in Japan. A middle school girl student then stood up to ask, "when on earth will Koreans stop their grumbling and complaints?" It is not impossible to imagine the background to her question if you see it as the result of almost no education in the modern history of Japan and Asia, but what really sticks in my mind, is her challenging tone, and the words "complaints and grievances." I was taken aback and can't even remember how I answered. Hearing a high school girl say the words "when on earth will ..." made me think of myself and other Koreans, and how often we would say "when on earth will discrimination cease?" On the train going home I felt like calling on the teachers and family of this girl.

---

3   Funding of the Christian pavilion by the Japanese Church of Christ at the Osaka Expo was provided against a background of controversy and protest over renewal of the Japan-US Security Treaty. Meetings were disruptive and violent, taken over by student radicals. Translator's note.

At the same time I remembered a bitter experience of racial and sexual discrimination that happened in our former church. It was an incident involving the Bishop of the church in which my husband, then fiancee, was a priest, and at the root of it was, in short, the Emperor system which had been grafted onto the Christian faith. At the time I married, the prayer book of the Japan Bible Society contained prayers for the Emperor (removed in 1988). My fiancee pointed out to the Bishop that there are problems with the quality of faith and churches which preserve discrimination, to which the bishop replied "the poor Emperor," shed some tears and ordered my husband to leave the church. I who had already resolved to leave anyway, saw parallels in our experience with the flight from Egypt. As Bishop of the Japan Bible Society he was a Japanese Christian male. The power of his faith in the emperor, the root cause of his racial and sexual discrimination - was greater than the power of his faith in Christ.

Now nearly fifty years since the end of the war, the 'word of God' as spoken at Japanese churches, theological colleges and mission schools, is again being used to disregard human dignity. I would not want this to ultimately become 'words of control' used by the strong to oppress the weak. Japan has again become a dominating country, riding a wave of high level economic growth after the Korean war, and the Osaka Exposition in 1970 provided the opportunity to launch a new invasion of Asia. If religious minority churches desire to be practising Christians according to the word of God and believe in loving their neighbour in such a society, there is no other path than to reflect on the present through history as spoken by Asian victims. Theology which speaks with no awareness of past history and is imbued with the consciousness of being an 'economic power,' will again become a tool of Japanese imperialism, and the brandishing of authority derived from an imperial state will result in forced assimilation again. What is more, quoting from the Bible as a means of silencing accusations of the oppressed and teaching to believe in the pain of social and political oppression as God's 'mercy', teaches an authority which is not actually the authority of God and enforces a double layer of discrimination.

It is important that we question Christian's historical understanding and the nature of theology and faith themselves, not only for Japanese Christians but also for myself as a Christian Korean woman in Japan. Christian Koreans, who are themselves a minority amongst the Korean minority in Japan, need to ask themselves about their historical understanding, what kind of theology they accept or reject, and how to base this in practice and faith which leads to liberation.

Japanese Koreans born of Japanese imperialism are caught between the three states of Japan, South and North Korea; they continue their struggle against discrimination from Japanese society, and the Emperor system which still dominates the centre of the structure of discrimination.

Finally, it is an historical fact that Emperor Hirohito was at the apex of the Japanese imperialism which gave birth to the comfort women problem. The fifteen year war was begun in the name of the Emperor, and terminated with the Emperors Broadcast. The Emperor, whose status had been that of a god, renounced divinity and 'peace and democracy' were preached, but what really became of that?

On reflection it is not only Christians, but the various religions of Japan which also cooperated wholeheartedly in the Asian war of aggression (although a minority did not), and the recognition of war responsibility is still also extremely weak. Has there been any sign of words or deeds to answer the historical pains of Asia evident in the crying voices of people who have been robbed of their humanity and those now dead. Still now the bitter voices of Asia are wandering the earth and calling, reaching down to their descendants. The life of the bitterness conceived inside my 2.5 generation body, has woken from thirty years of sleeping oppression - and I am now sounding out a cry of 'liberation!'

Afterword - The Future of Feminism and Religion

Okano Haruko

Religion has deep connections to the ideologies of the several processes of civilisation and modernisation - questions of significance and scale apart - which Japan has undergone in the past. Shinto and Buddhism played definitive roles in centralisation through the Emperor and implementation of the *ritsuryo* system of centralised autocracy, while Confucianism was similarly important in establishing so-called modern feudalism. Then again in the Meiji Restoration, Shinto had a central role through direct Imperial rule. There was no shadow of religion, however, in the rebirth of modernisation which occurred in the process of regeneration and democratisation after losing the second world war. As I discussed in 'A Feminist Critique of Japanese Religions,' with the exception of the period after the war, religion was used to justify strengthening the system and *ie* in tandem with modernisation, while negative factors such as sexual discrimination and class discrimination also increased in direct proportion. Does this mean then, that such absurd discrimination is perhaps inherent in religion?

Religion can be thought of as consisting of two parts. The first part is encountered through experiencing 'holiness' and 'absoluteness'. Through encounters with 'holiness,' one's own existence and the world as it has been until then, are negated, and there is a stage of feeling that a new self is prescribed. When human beings have a sense of being worked on by holiness, they begin to further respond to it. This is the second part. Feminist theologians have also recognised that Jesus Christ's consciousness of being a messiah clearly shaped his rejection of class, race and sexual discrimination in teaching the word of God. Contempt for and exclusion of women begins when this second part becomes part of tradition. In short, the tradition which includes editing of the Bible and formal ceremonies comes from a phase when it was formed with men at the centre.

The fact that Buddha rejected the caste system is well-known. The question of sexual discrimination, however, is a delicate one. In early Buddhist literature, hostility towards sex arose from an ascetic mentality which became one with hostility towards the female sex itself. This is evident from the phrases contemptuous of women that were incorporated into texts, the eight precepts that were laid down for Buddhist nuns, and the hesitation of Buddha to admit women to the first sect. The core of Buddha's teachings was to surmount life's attachments. More and more women nevertheless took shelter in a new life; but for them, Buddha was the origin of suffering, the prime mover in forming the object and desire of human existence, and was probably regarded as an awesome power of life. The power of women's sexuality, which is connected to giving birth to new life, is like a double-edged sword; highly regarded in terms of worldly values, but for inexperienced novices en route to emancipation from worldly attachments, it fans the flames of a burning attachment to life and is an obstacle that makes everything end in nought. This is because of the domination of the archaic perception that 'life' is in short 'sexuality.' The ambiguity of Buddha freely associating with prostitutes whilst also preaching the danger of women to his disciples, appears to stem from such a duality in perceptions of women. Buddha simply taught the sublation of suffering, mastering the road to salvation, and expelled everything that was not essential to the life of a seeker after truth. He refused, for example, to speculate on spirits of the afterworld, by teaching that a man hit by a poison arrow ought to extract the arrow, not seek the perpetrator.

Unlike Jesus Christ, who relativised a worldly value system while accepting victims of discrimination, including women, a revolutionary design that would turn traditional Hindu society's view of women around 180 degrees perhaps cannot be expected from Buddha's radical religious orientation. "The people who ride such a vehicle, be they man or woman, will truly reach nirvana" (Zoagon Sutra 22, So'o Section, the Taisho Tripitaka, No. 2. 156a). Nevertheless, these words of Buddha's should be considered as clearly expressing the starting point of Buddhism. And because the principle of exclusion is inevitably part of this base, there is of course in a male-centred world already a foundation to which sexual discrimination is easily tied. The notorious 'five female hindrances' and 'henjonanshi' arose as an ideology of sexual discrimination out of the process of establishing Mahayana Buddhism, and Buddhism's functioning as a universal religion. The experiences of religious figures who have relativised an existential system of values and state of the self through encounters with holiness, are before long put into words by disciples, then a tradition is formed and disseminated universally through organised proselytising. In any religion, the same kinds of problems arise in this second part, which regulates the essential nature of religion. When experiences are transformed into the written word, the original flexibility of the dynamic characteristic is lost and it comes to hold authority as rigid and static doctrine.

Furthermore, tenets and tradition were popularised so as to be easily comprehended based on the moral justification of achieving salvation for even just one more person. However there is a contradiction inherent in this because the sense of distance and relativity to the holy and sacred that is the starting point of religious experience, is weakened whilst internalising religious principles that have been popularised, thus simultaneous assimilation and acceptance of popular values is unavoidable. Becoming tied to the establishment is also, unfortunately, inevitable in the process of universalising religion; that is to say, it is when the interests of both sides coincide. Therefore the ethnic religion Shinto, which originally did not have a spirit of negating reality or the necessity of universalisation, also did not have the internal dilemmas of universal religions, and hence could be linked to the establishment. I believe that the key to solving many of the problems of feminism lies in analyzing the complex processes of modernisation in society and religion.

What were the benefits for us of the post-war modernisation which deprived religions of their distinctive colours?

The various global problems spawned by highly industrialised society - environmental destruction, increased armaments, inequalities between advanced and developing countries, etc. - are becoming more acute day by day. Open sexual discrimination such as the exclusion of women is decreasing, but consciousness of the gender-based division of roles is firmly rooted, and in many areas of life women are still the weaker party. There have also been offensive comments such as 'if it is evident that a child has a major disability the parent should not give birth to that child,' coming from the mouths of people designated as cultural figures. As I mentioned previously, the maternal principle which permeates Japanese society encompasses only a homogeneous group. Different people are perceived as strange, while the weak are seen as a burden on society and are isolated on the margins of the community. Charitable work by the magnanimous will not truly liberate women, the weak, those who drop out of society or who are are forced to drop out. The universal religious principle of salvation which aids all fellowship is supposed to play that role. On that premise, religion restores the power of liberation. It is also connected to the question of how to recover that which was lost in the process of religion becoming sectarian, universalised and popularised.

In short, it is bringing into the present the experience of encountering holiness, the starting point of religion, and restoring the dynamism to pursue a change of values in a society governed by wealth and power. In this way we ought to be able to learn how truly relative our existence is. Only by recognising this relativity can we foster the morality to enable tolerance of others way of life, including the weak.

In any culture or religion, the easily committed erroneous and intolerant assertion that only oneself is in possession of the absolute truth, is born of an immature mentality which has not learned through experience the relativity of human beings. Maternal Japanese society, which would have it that only the same kind of people can live together, is likewise immature because of this absolute view of its own homogeneity. The homogeneous principle of an archaic communal structure should, through once being negated, be able to accept differences and be turned around into a mature community spirit.

In a report entitled 'Future Economy and Labor,' The Japan Federation of Employers' Associations stressed that "people-focused management must not change," to which one female industrialist made a very interesting refutation. "This is nothing more than the 'principle of employee focus.' When, as in western industry, various human resources such as women, the aged, foreigners, and the handicapped are embraced, only then can it be called human-centred." (Asahi Shimbun, morning edition, 21 August 1992). This criticism adroitly puts a finger on the fundamental immaturity of closed Japanese society. The Japanese nation which currently encompasses people of many different cultures, cannot continue to continue clinging to this idea of homogeneity. The sense of crisis spreading across the world, is not coming from the energy of a homogeneous society, but is called up by the altruism of a mature society. In this, the dynamism of the universal religions of Buddhism and Christianity to change values at an individual and social level, present a model.

In Buddhism for example, human existence and way of life is relativised by preaching that all phenomena, including human existence, is nothing more than a temporary assembly of mind and matter. Therefore a change of values occurred whereby the lifestyles of 'leaving home' and 'mendicancy' were chosen as the best route for deliverance. Instead of dismantling the consanguinary *ie*, Buddhism bound separate individuals together in a spiritual communal structure through its teaching of the altruistic path of Buddha's compassion and bodhisattva's altruistic path.

In the same way, Christianity also teaches that the true family community lies beyond the ties of flesh and blood. "My mother and my brethren are these which hear the word of God, and do it" (Luke chp.8, verse 21). The bonds of this spiritual family which Jesus Christ spoke of, encompass not only the love of God and neighbours, but also enemies, and is realised through the mutual love of each member.

The 'compassion' of Buddhism and 'love' of Christianity - principles which have secured a spiritual community presented by universal religions, have been manipulated by a machine civilisation, the heated competition of industry and education, and the endless consumerism and waste of modern society - do they not have an important meaning? The causes of spiritual anguish in children, who must bear the burdens of the next generation, should not be blamed on mothers alone, nor on absent fathers. In the background of young mothers struggling to bring up children alone, and men becoming industrial warriors and dying of overwork - all cases cannot be mentioned - there is an immaturity in the consciousnesses of both husbands and wives who are content with their division of roles by gender. Raising children and education are the woman's job, while the man's role is to succeed and get ahead in society; this myth of role divisions has been woven as a spell into a common understanding which now needs to be re-examined. The development of mass transport and communication has increasingly brought people of different cultures in contact with each other. When the various authorities and powers who dehumanise people and oppress humanity are overthrown, and each person can acknowledge others' characters and way of living, then in order to create mutual relations that will help others become better people, feminism and religion must be able to construct anthropologies from a global perspective, which incorporate diverse models.

Authors

Okano Haruko

Born 1941. Graduated from Bonn University. Doctor of Philosophy. Professor at Jissen Women's University. Specialist in comparative religion. Author of "Women in Shinto History" (in German, Harrassowitz). Co-author of "Japan and Germany - Women's New Wave" (in Japanese, Kawai Shuppan) and others.

Kono Nobuko

Born 1927. Women's issues critic. Author of "History of Modern Women's Spirituality" (in Japanese, Daiwa Shobo), "Woman of the Fire Country - Takamure Itsue," "The Family Illusion" (both in Japanese, Shinhyoron), "The Tale of A Hidden Village" (Sanichi Shobo) and many others.

Nakano Yuko

Born 1961. Completed doctoral thesis in Buddhist studies at Komazawa University. Specializes in women's studies, Buddhist studies, religious anthropology and ethnology. Researcher at the Soto Sect Research Institute. Author of the paper "Aspects of Sexual Discrimination in Japanese Buddhism - Focusing on the Soto Sect" (in Japanese) and many others.

Iwata Sumie

Born 1937. Graduated from International Christian University. Head of the National Christian Council in Japan's Centre for Christian Response to Asian Issues. Paper on "Firm Steps Towards Peace - With the Quakers," translator of "The Church and the Second Sex" (Miraisha).

Okuda Akiko

Born 1938. Graduated from International Christian University. Editor of "Women Have Written" (in Japanese, Kei Shobo). Translator of "History of the Jewish People" (Sanichi Shobo), co-translator of "Women's Liberation and Christianity" (Shinkyo Shuppansha), "Another Me" (Gakuseishorin) and many others.

Igeta Midori

Born 1946. Doctorate from the Tokyo University Department of Humanities. Lecturer at University of the Sacred Heart. Specializes in Religious studies. Co-author of "Contemporary Religious Studies 4" (Tokyo University Press), translator of "Learning from Death" (Hozokan) and others.

Haga Akira

Born 1927. Freelance writer writing on the topics of feminism, space, religion as the ultimate of life, peace stemming from conquering of the ego.

Chun Kwangne

Born 1956. Completed part of doctorate at Tokyo Union Theological Seminary. Interested in Confucianism, discrimination against women and ethnic minorities in Canadian society.

Translator

Alison Watts

Born in Australia1963. Graduated from the University of Adelaide and Flinders University, Australia. English teacher in China, Australia and Japan. Freelance translator since 1993, specializing in human rights and women's issues.